VIVID IMAGINATION

By
Benjamin Allen

"The Painter's Tale" Written by Gia'na Maya Garel
Copyright©2015 GM Garel

Published by Portraits That Breathe
www.Portraitsthatbreath.com

Printed in the United States of America

Copyright © 2015 by Benjamin Allen
ISBN-13: 978-1503022676
ISBN-10: 1503022676

ART CONTENTS
(PICTURES IN ORDER OF APPEARANCE)

GOLD TEX
HORIZON
DEEPLY ROOTED
RISE ABOVE THE SURFACE
GOLD MINE
HIDDEN TREASURES
COLOR MASH
SUNNY SIDE UP
APPLE SWIRL
FACE PAINT
SIMPLY GREEN
BLINK OF AN EYE
DAPPER BLUE
CONCEPTS OF COLOR
STONE WASH
SWEET TOOTH
TOUGH SKIN
Q BALL
AUTUMN MELTDOWN
MAN BEHIND THE MASK 1
THINKING MAN ("THE PAINTER'S TALE")
LIONHEARTED

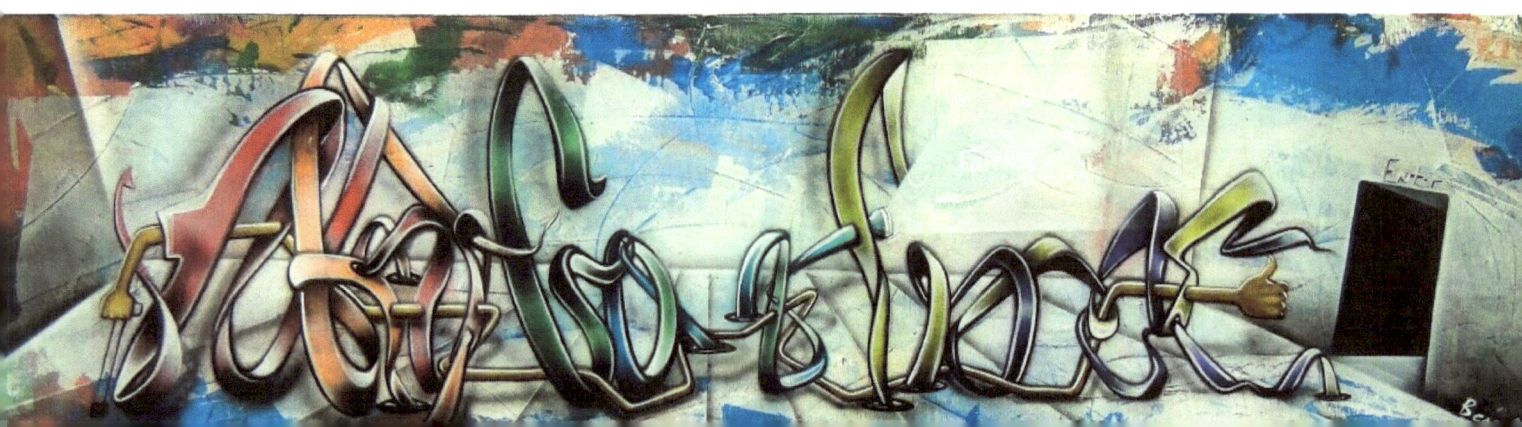

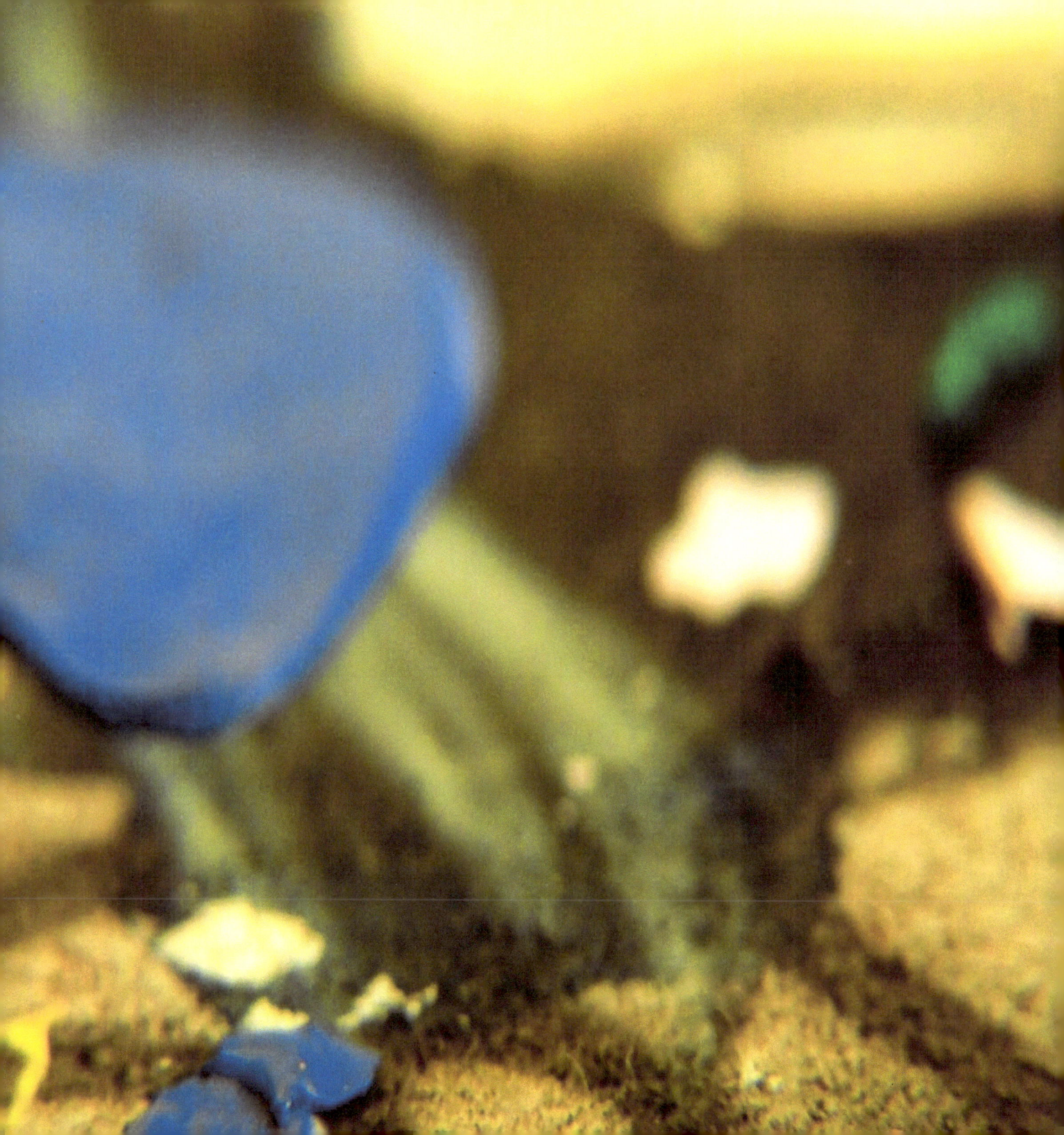

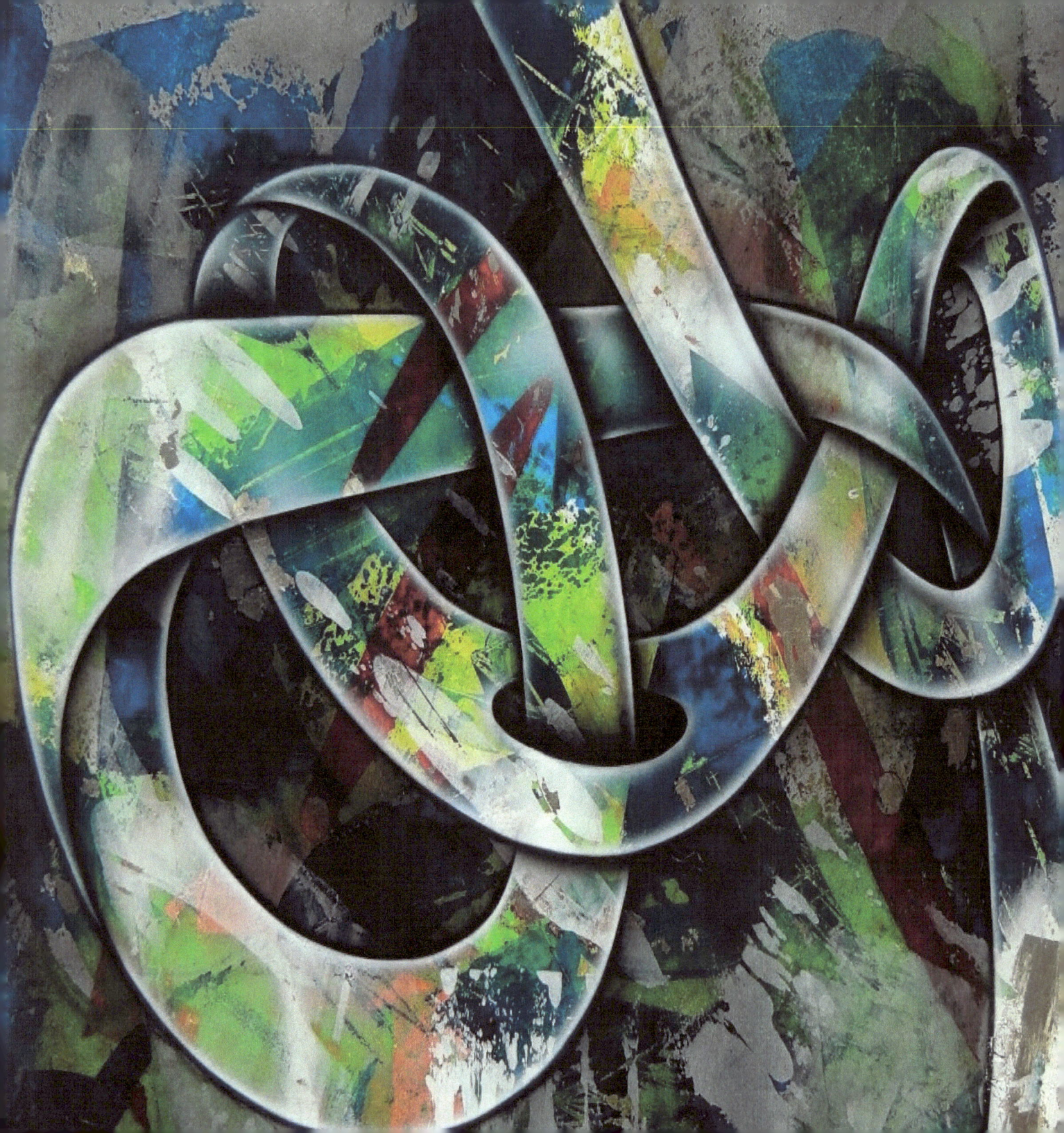

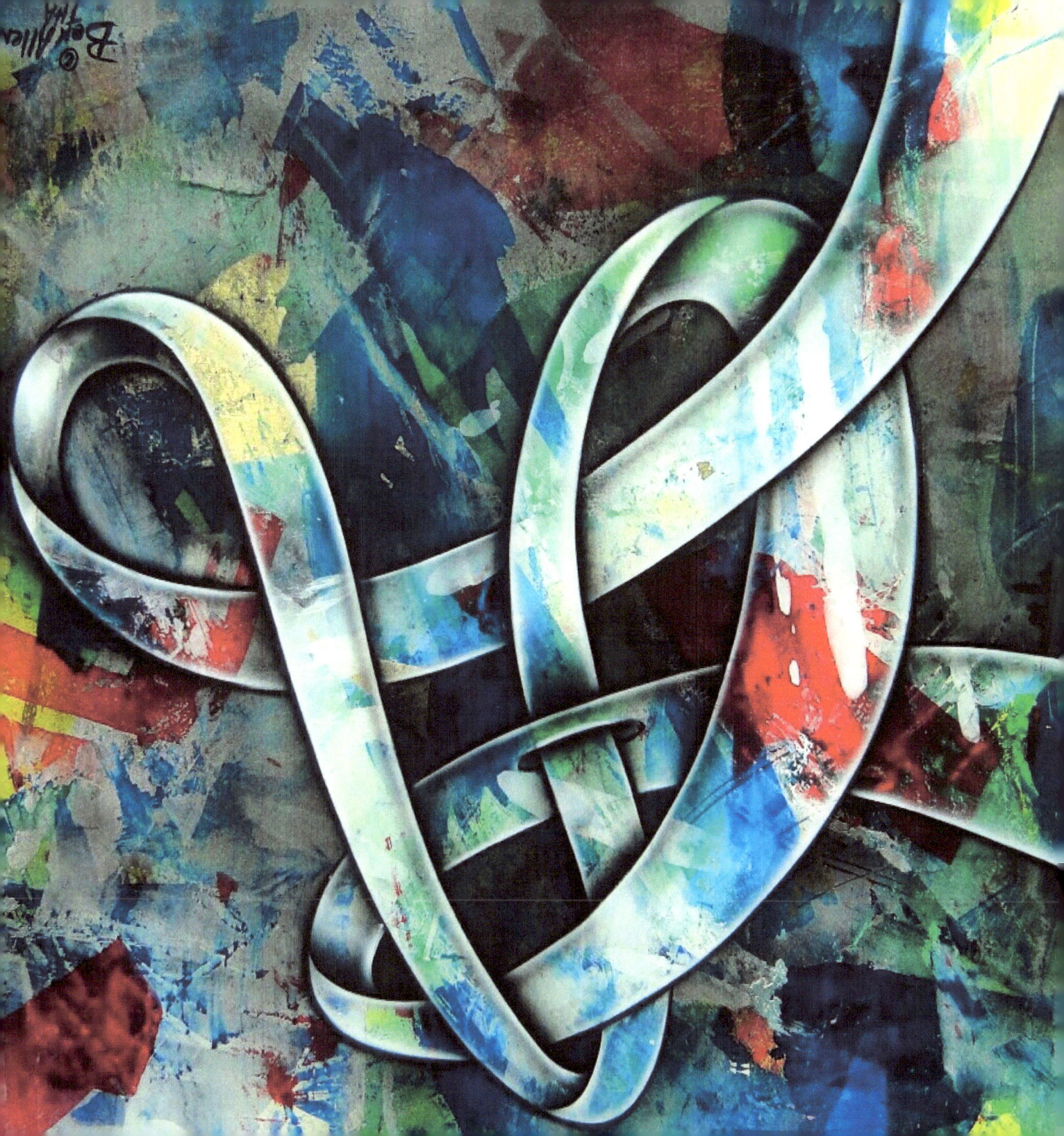

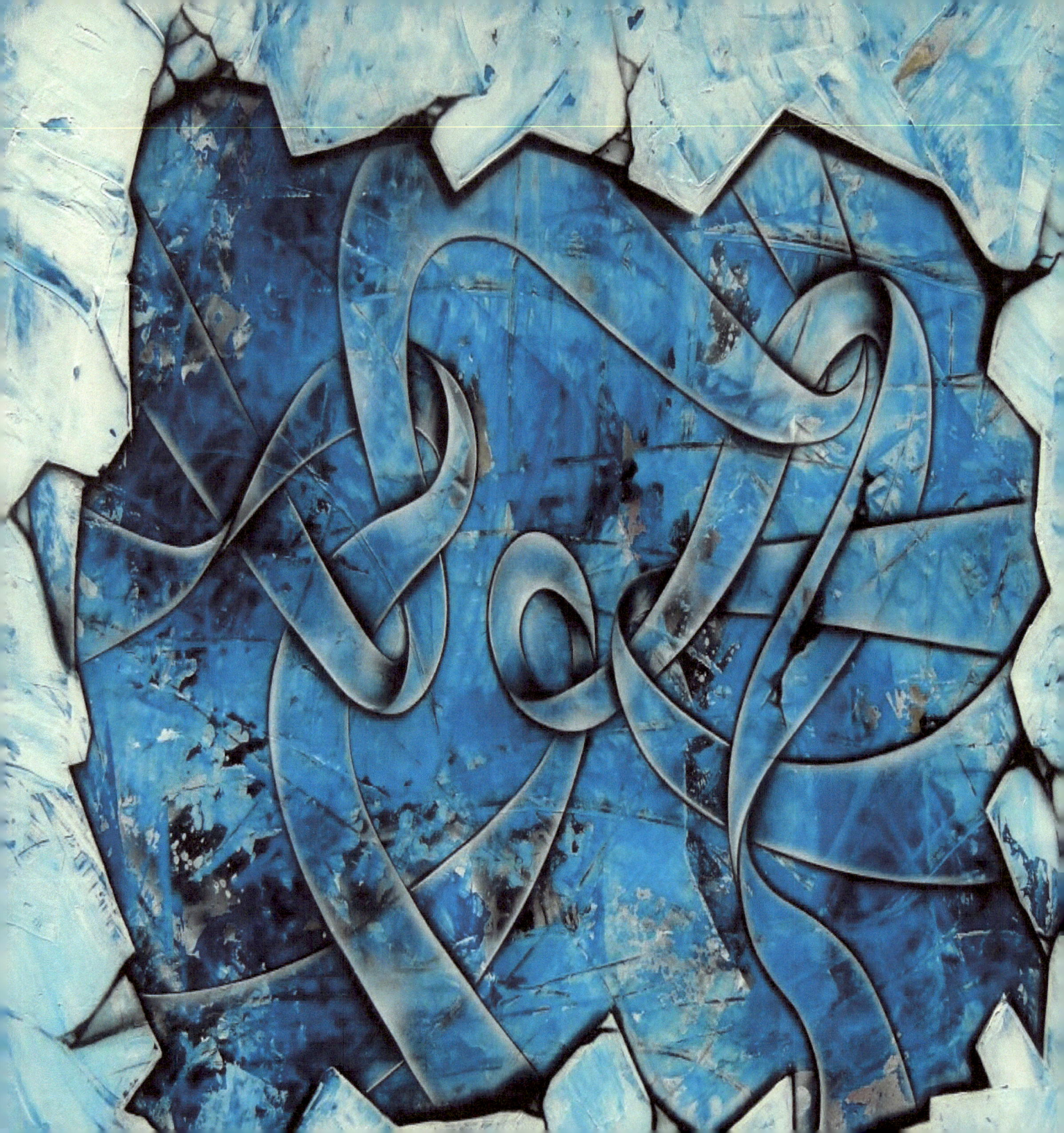

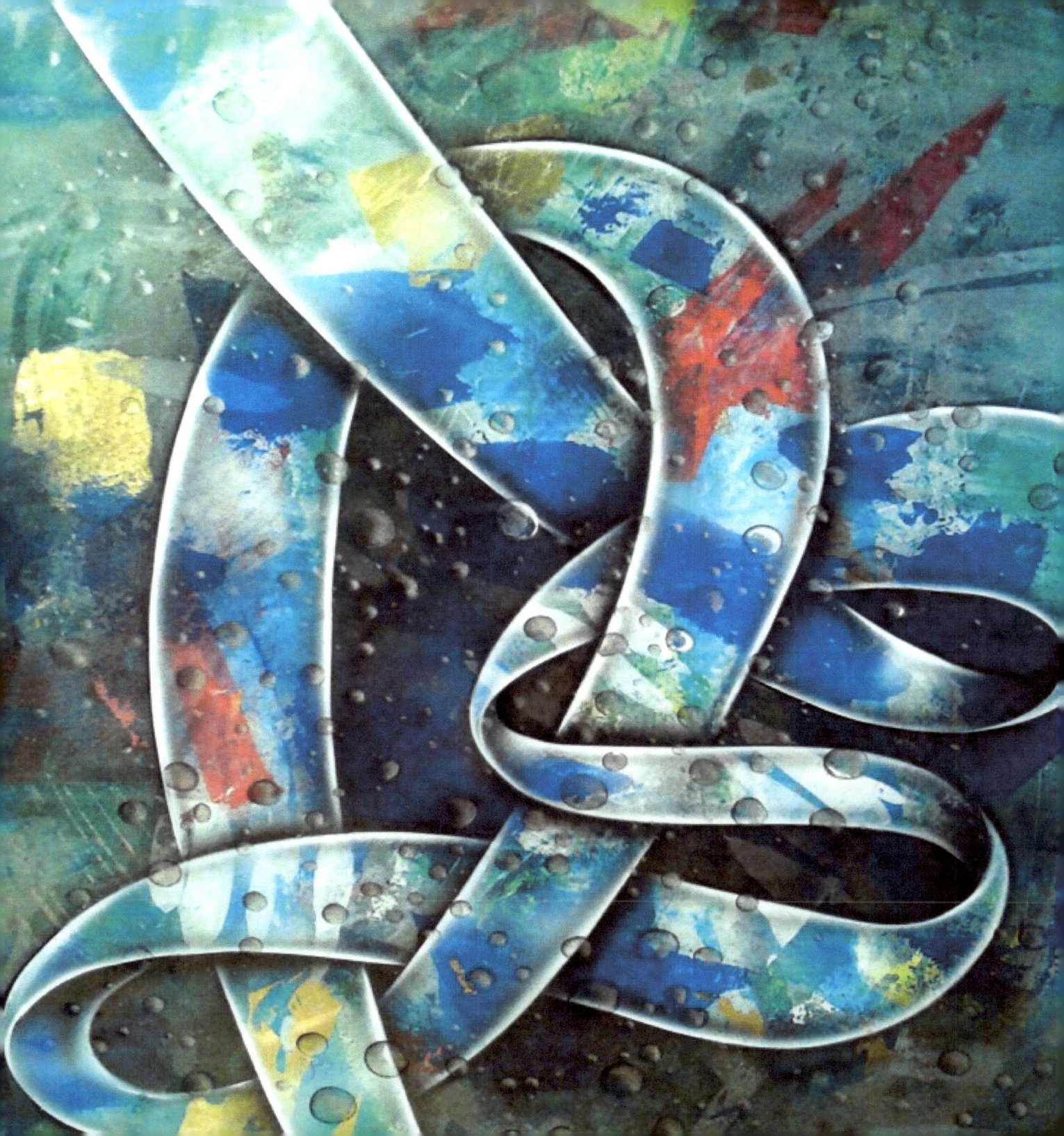

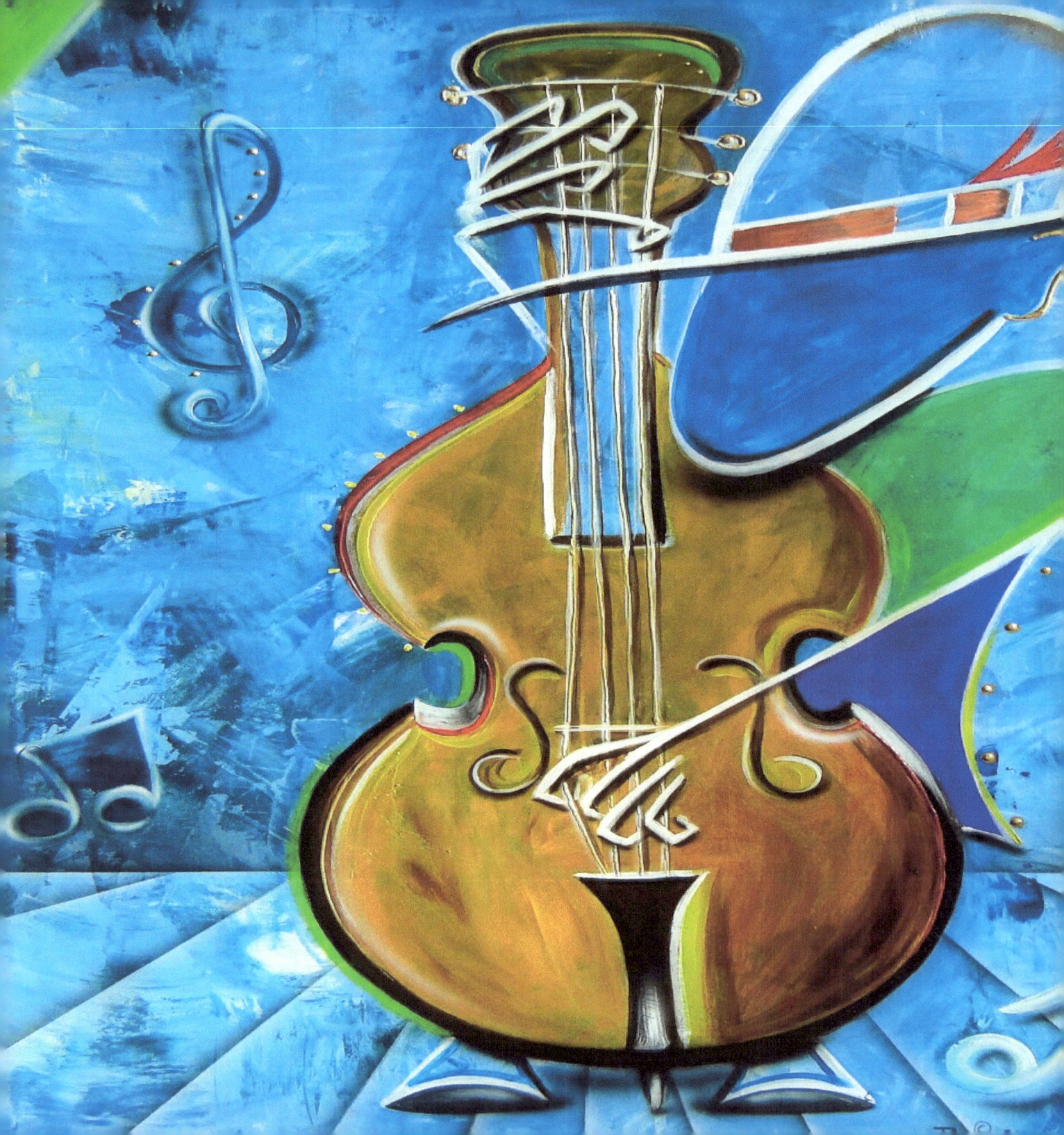

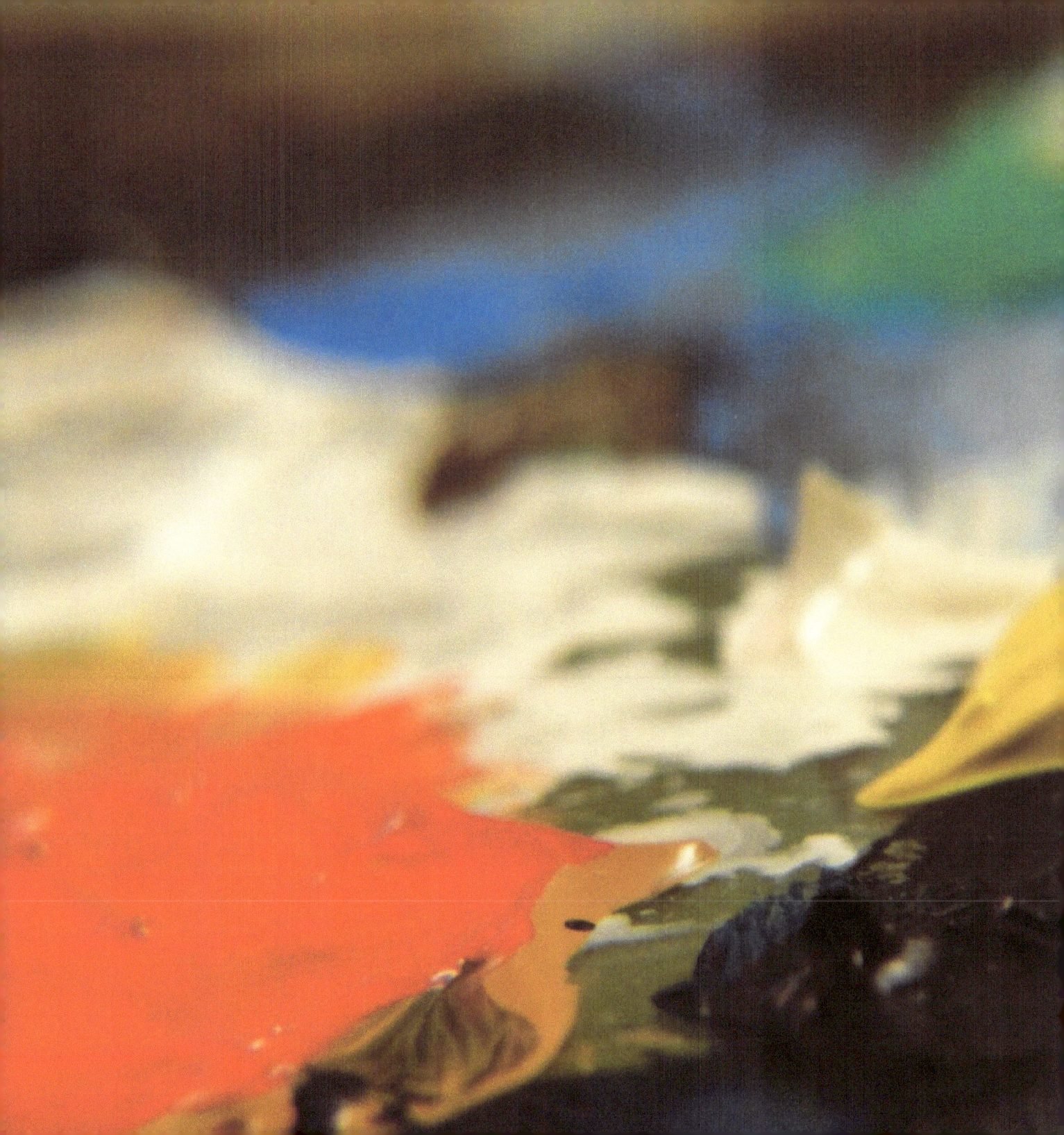

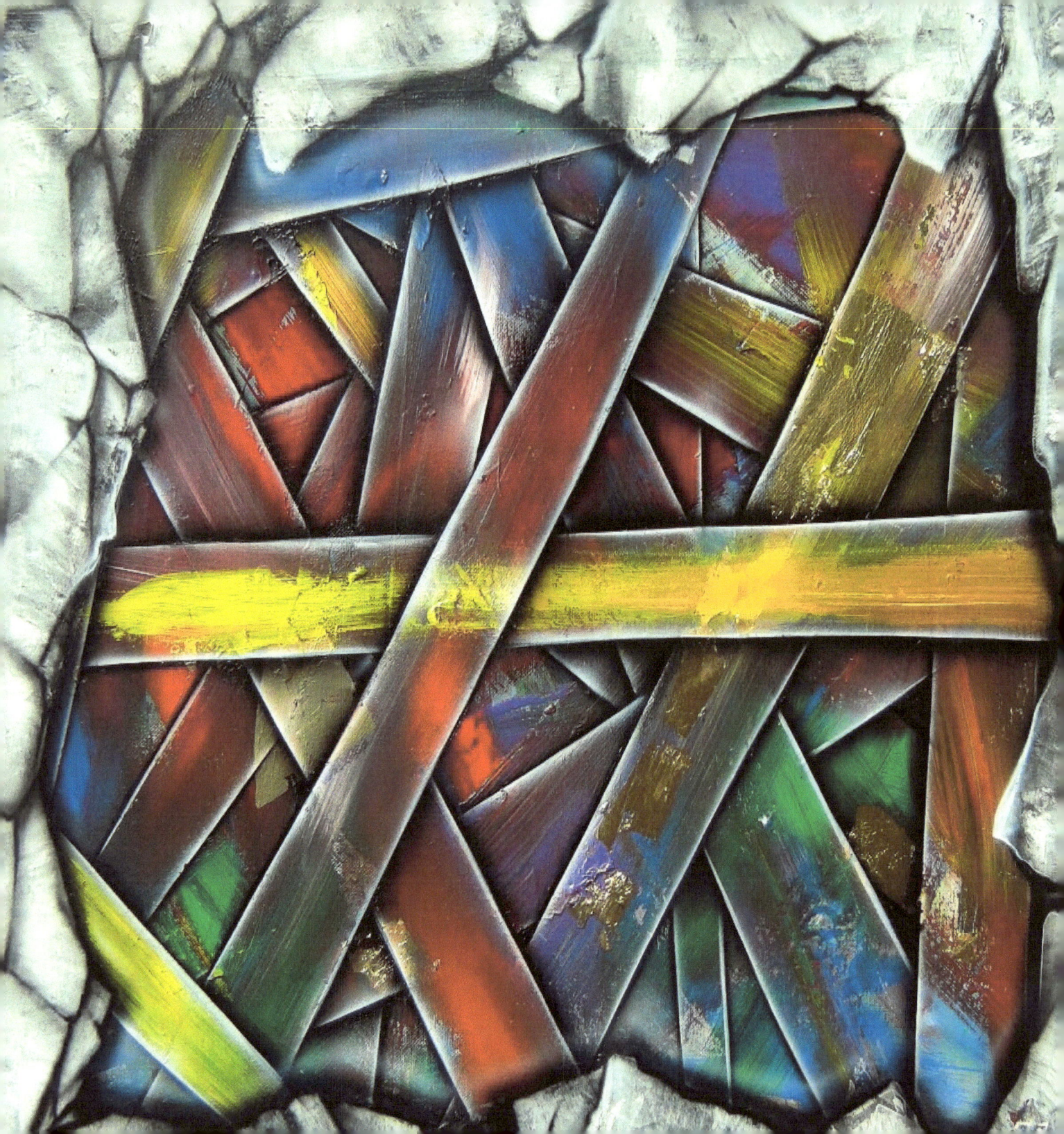

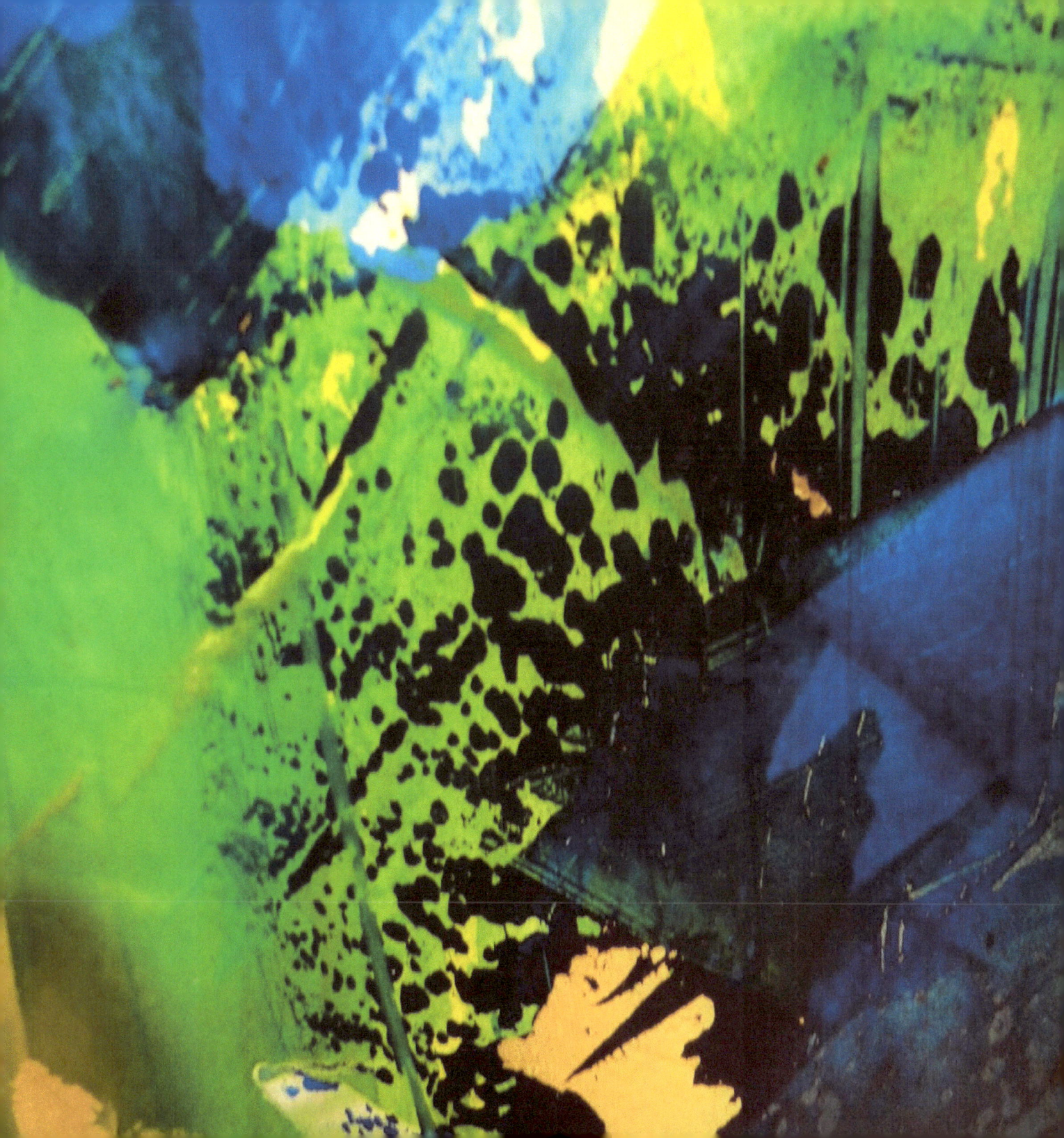

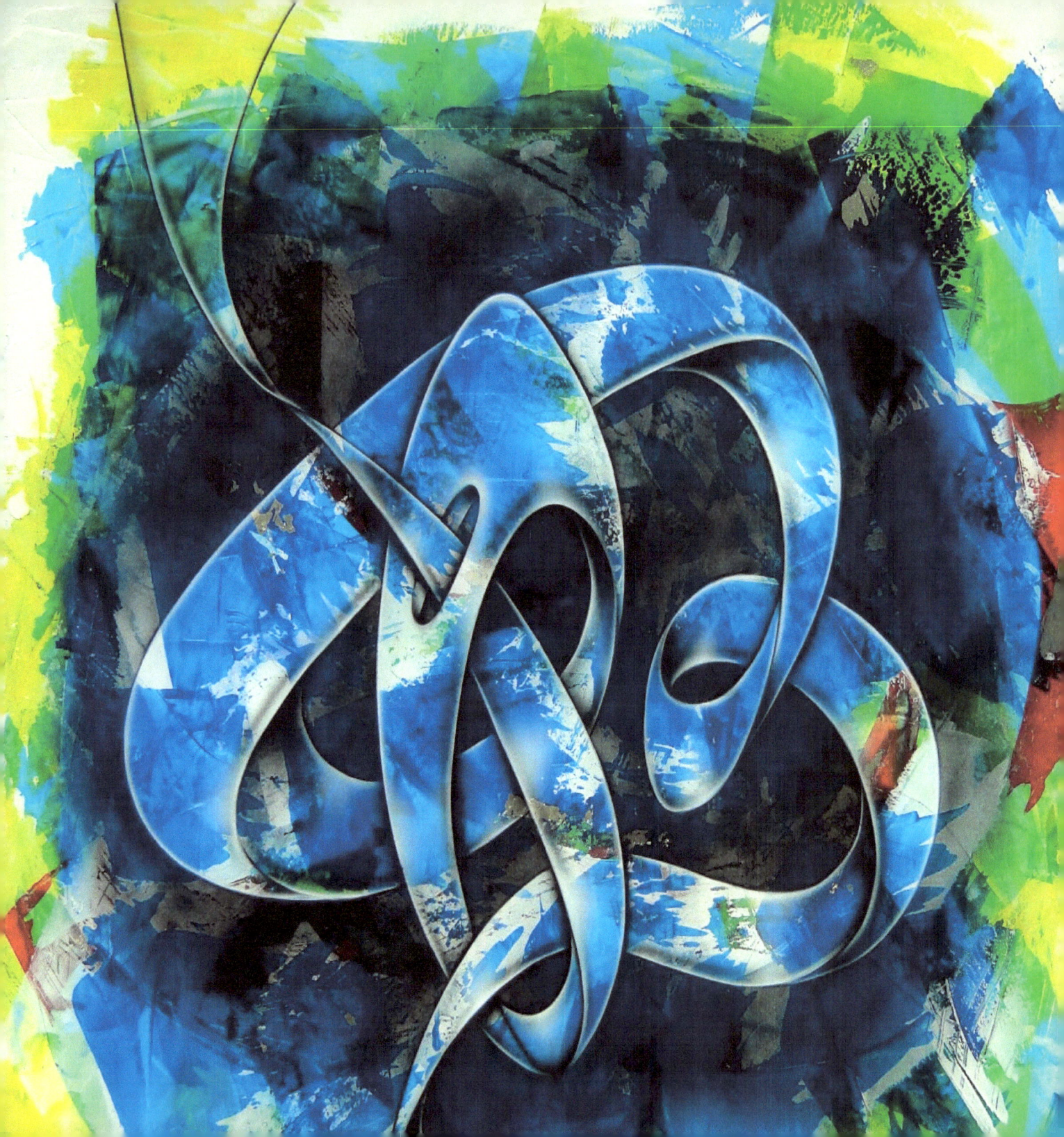

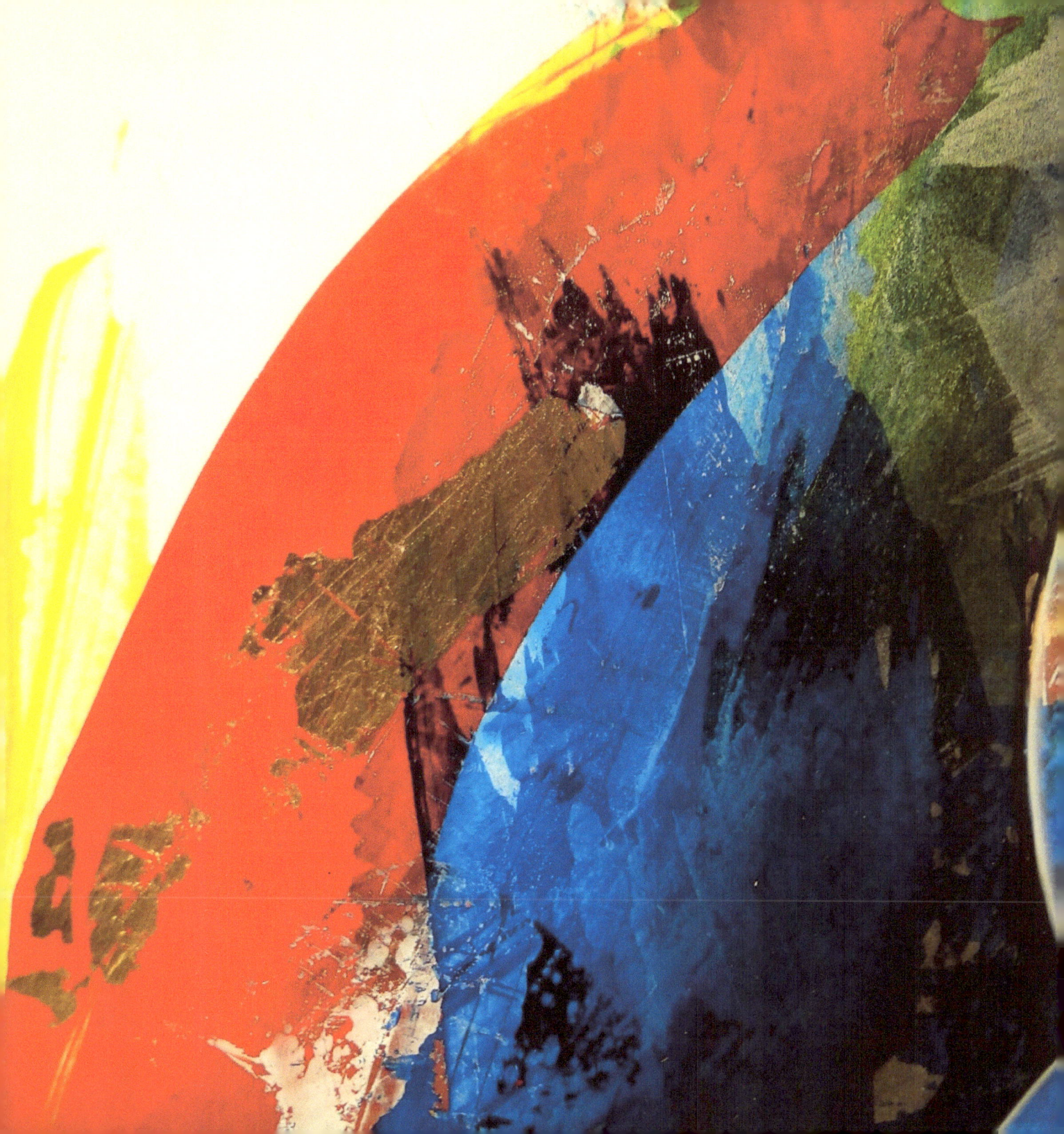

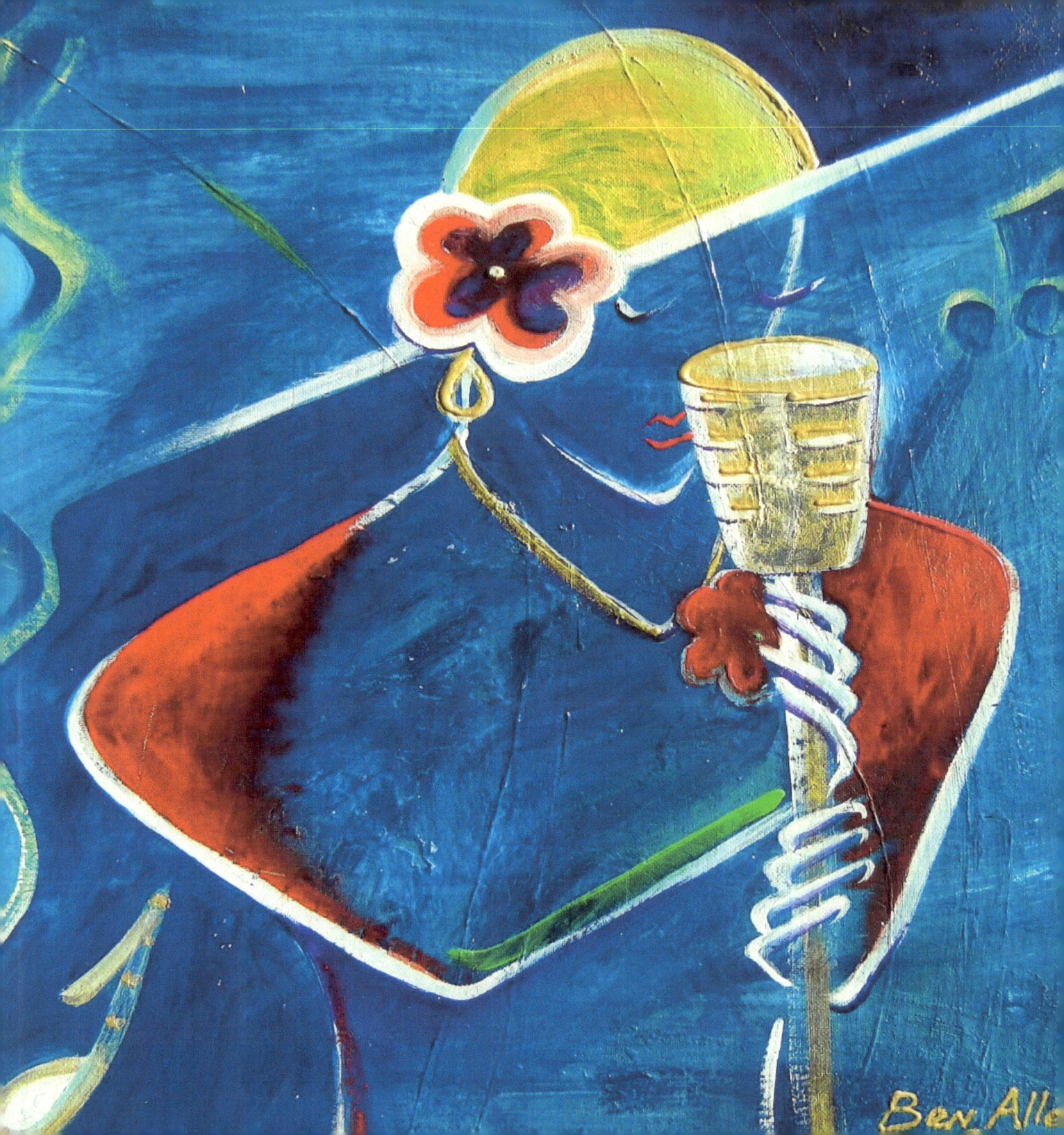

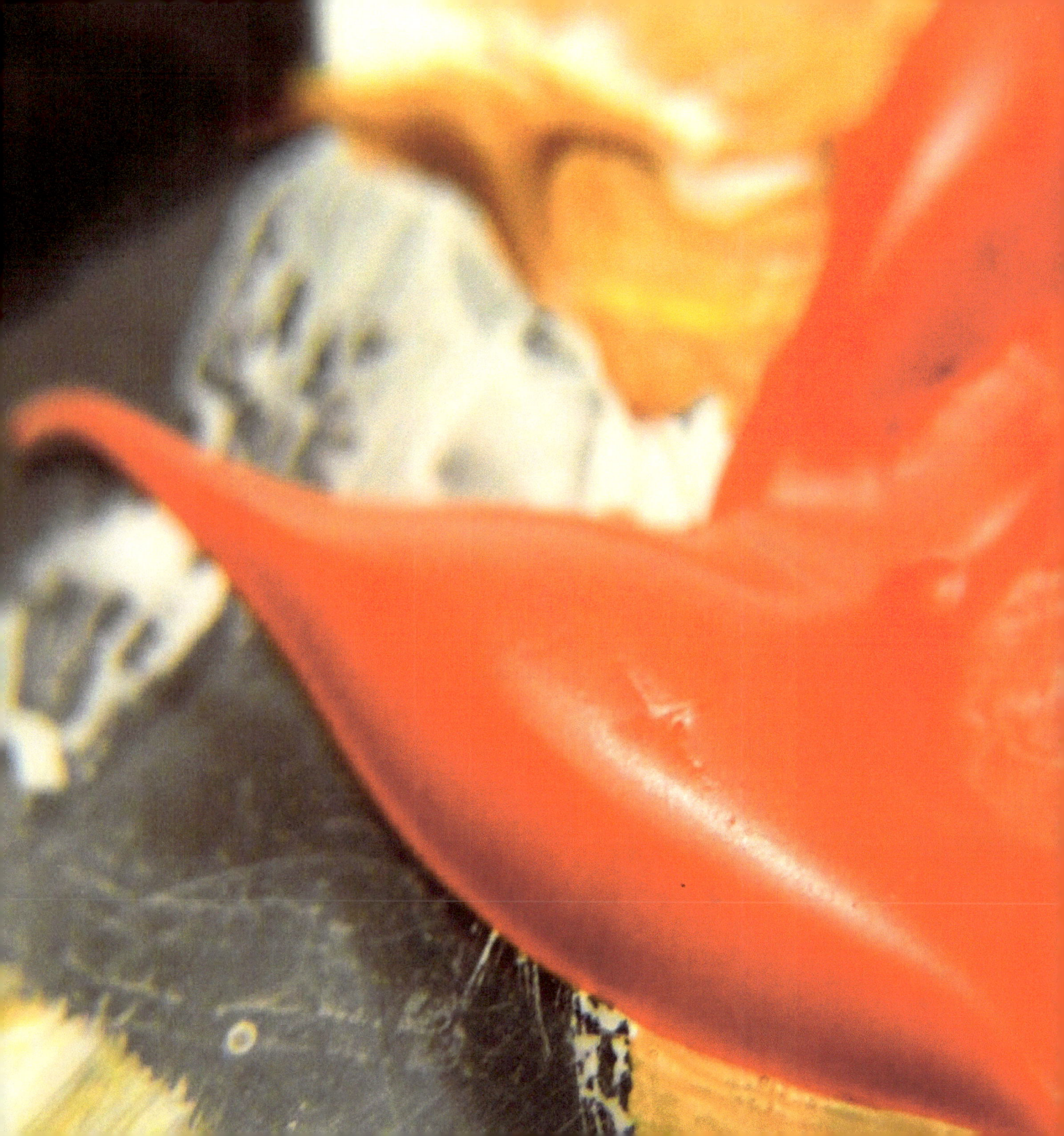

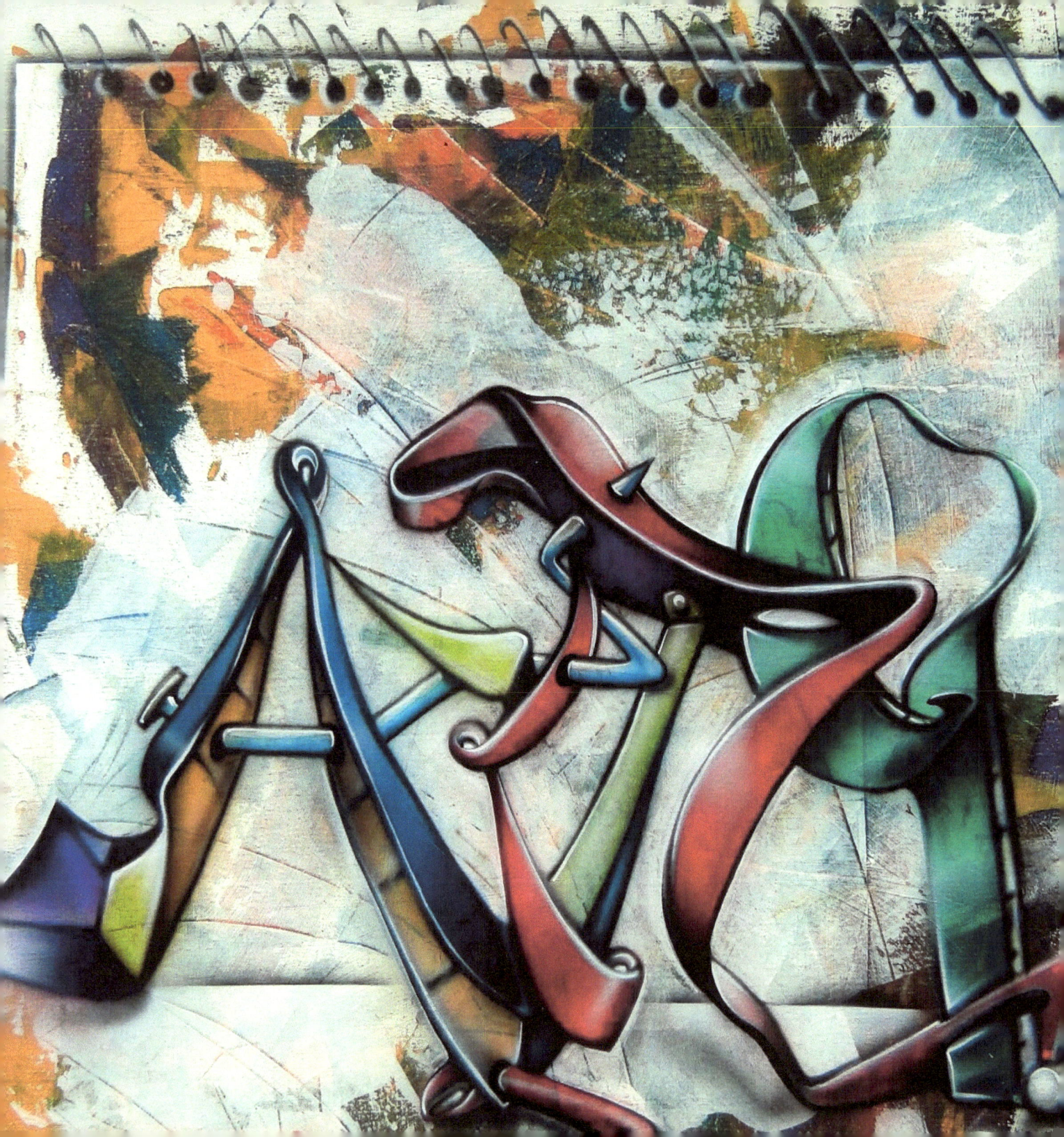

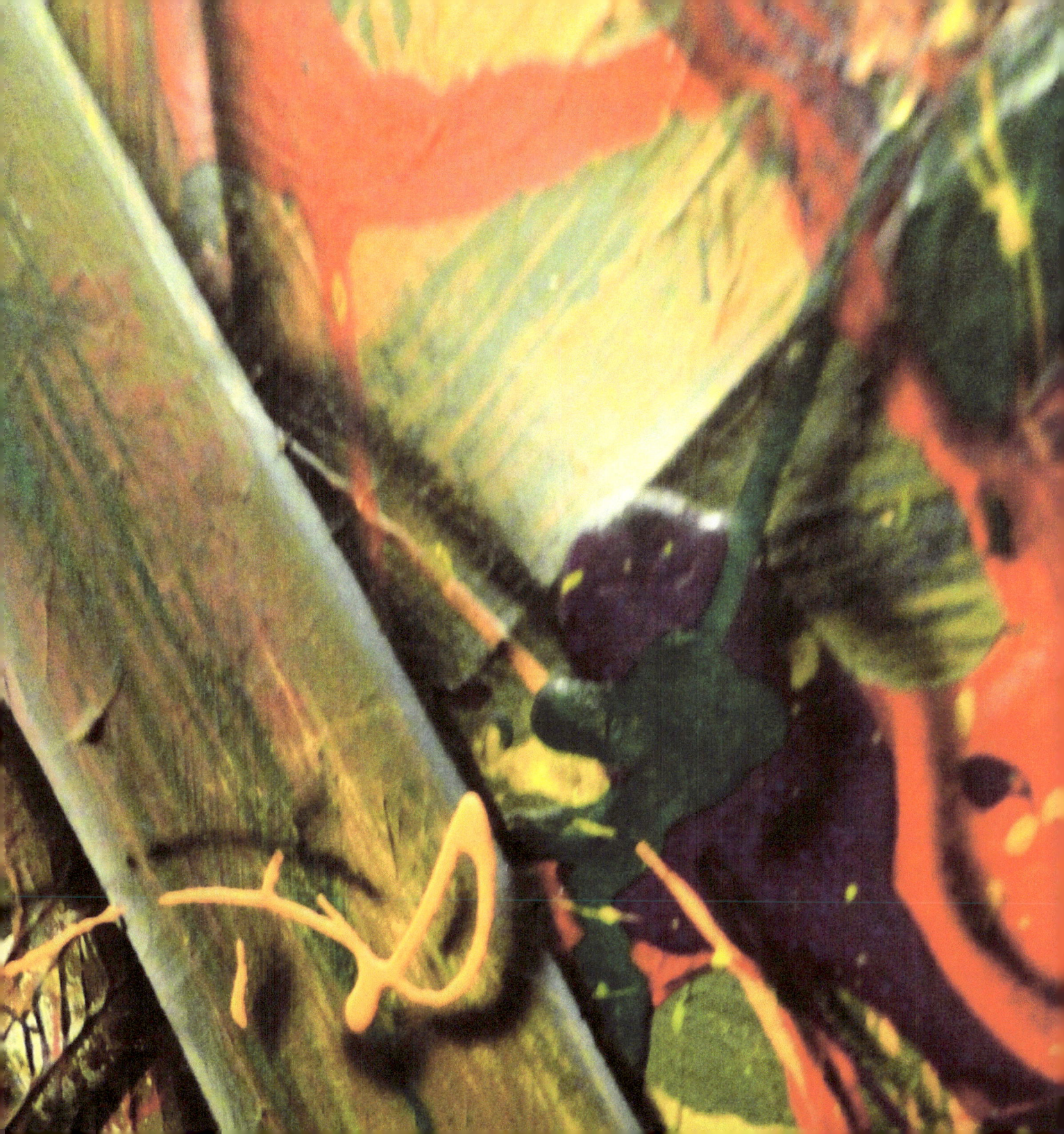

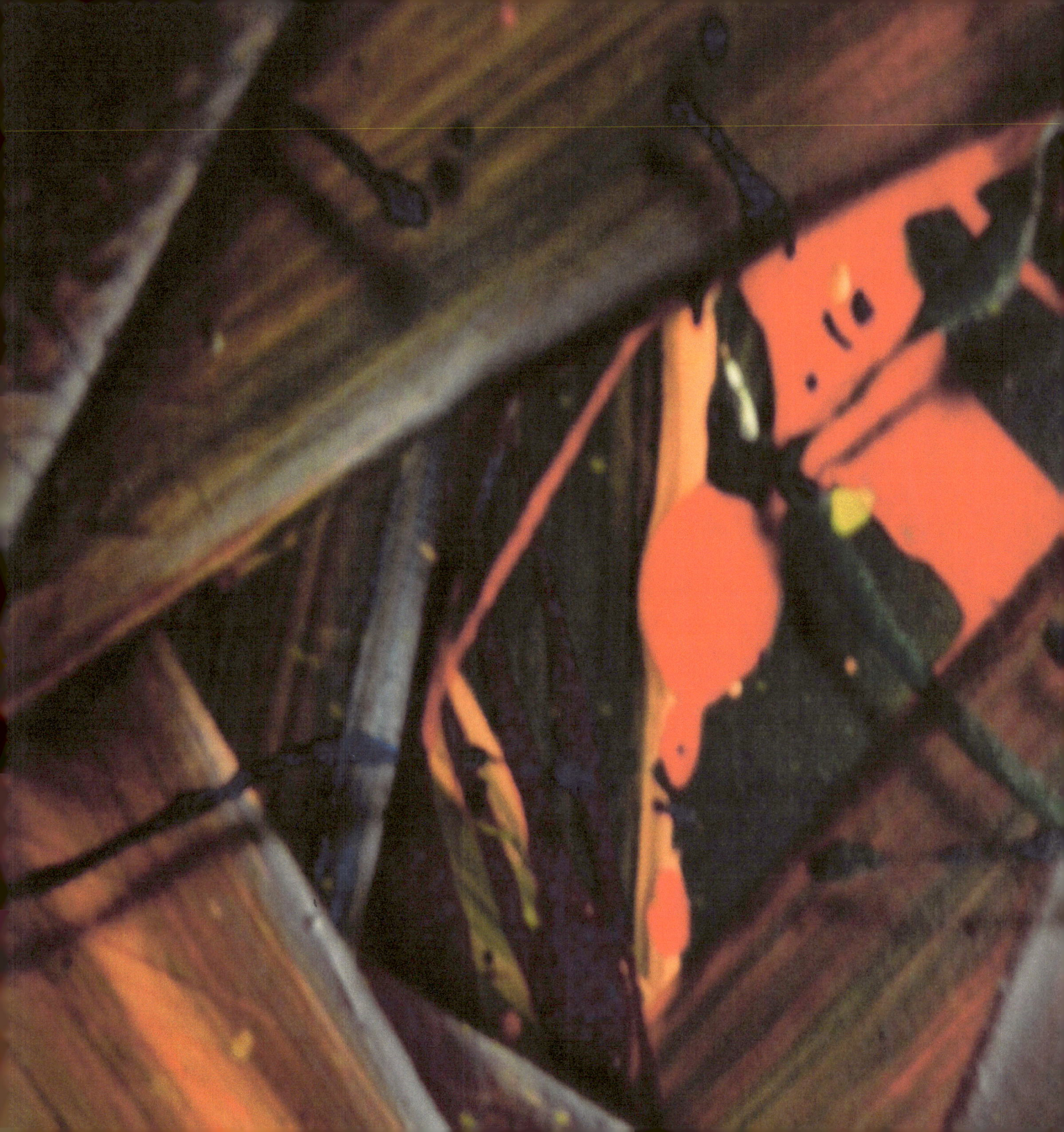

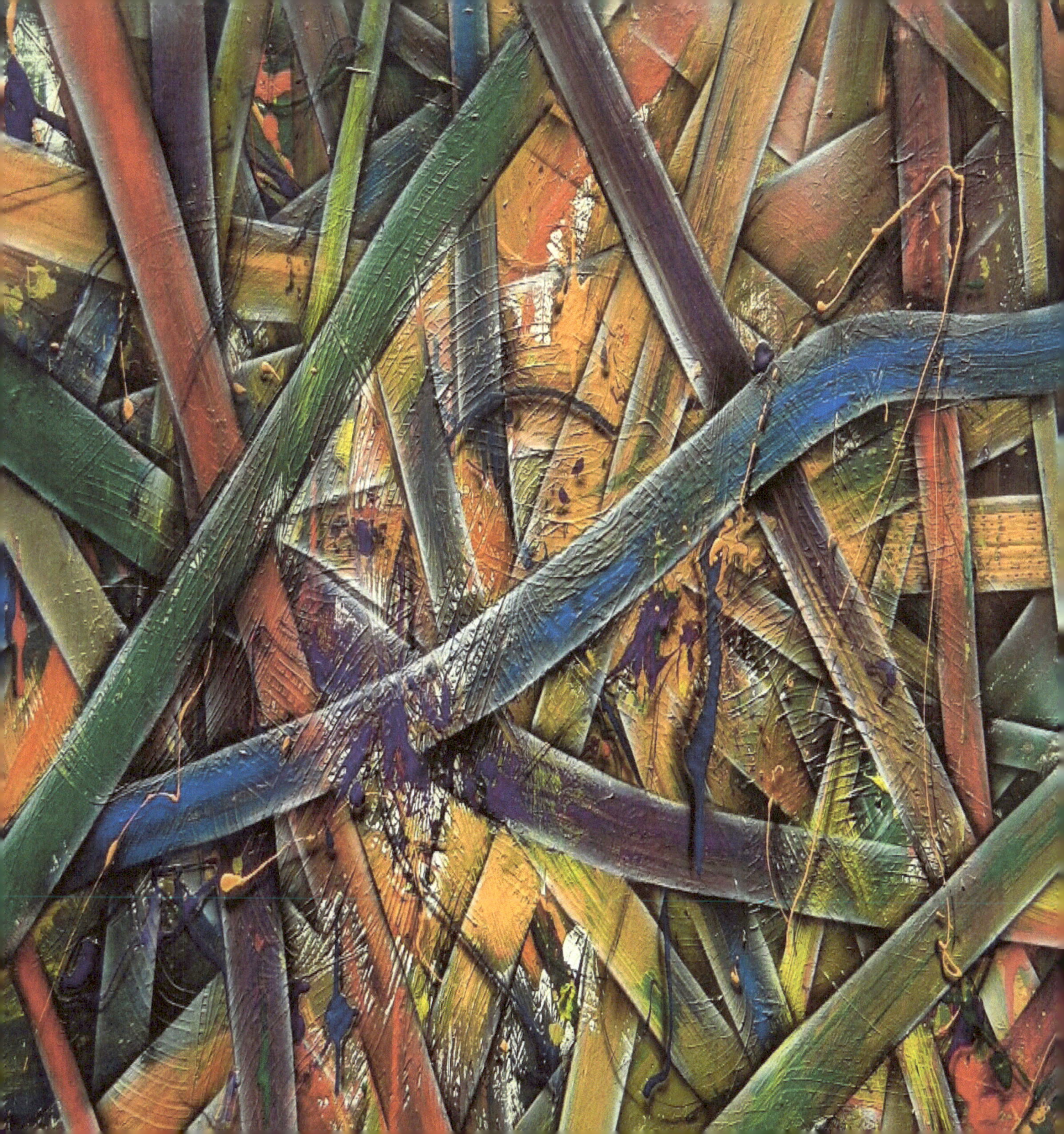

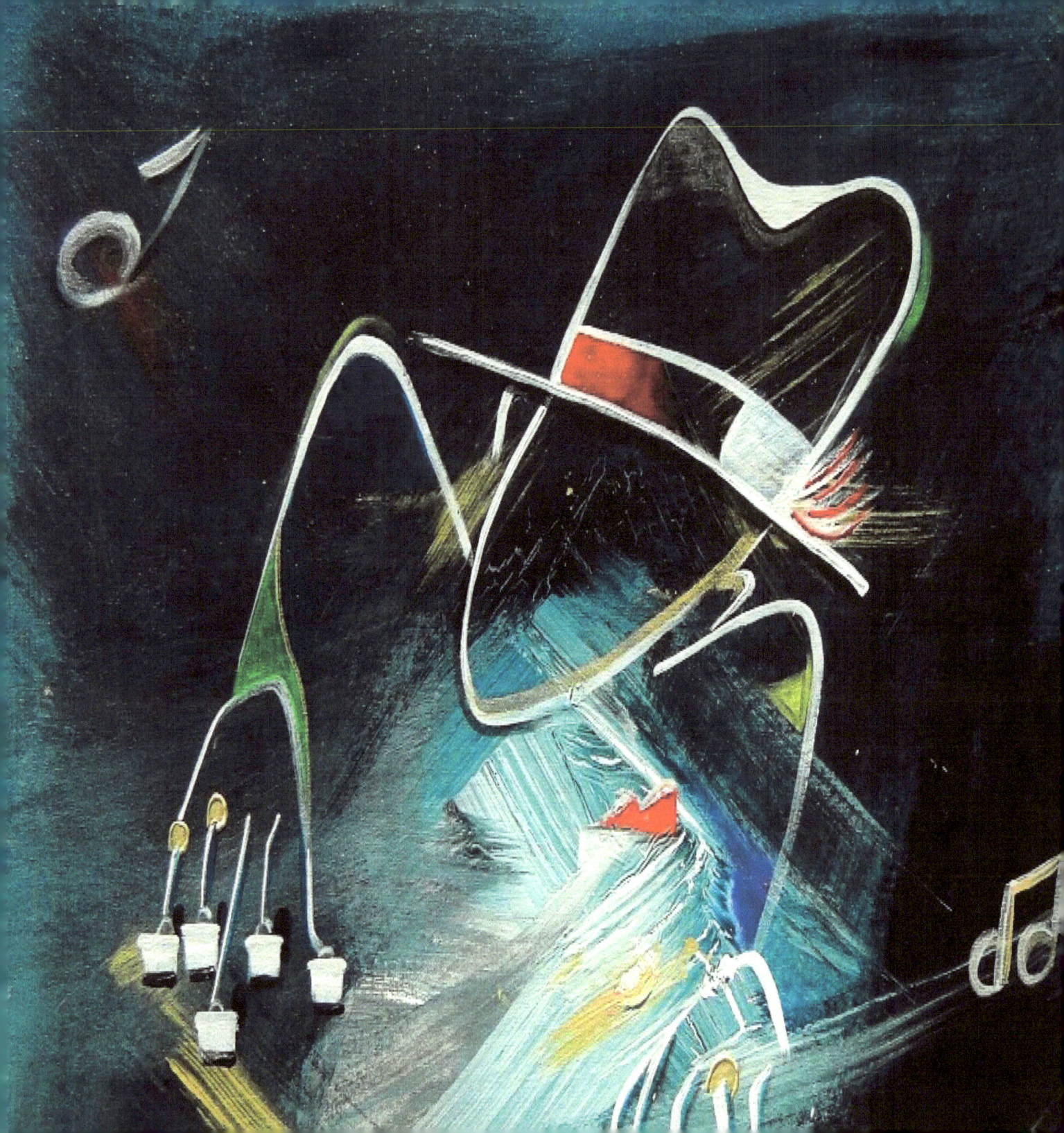

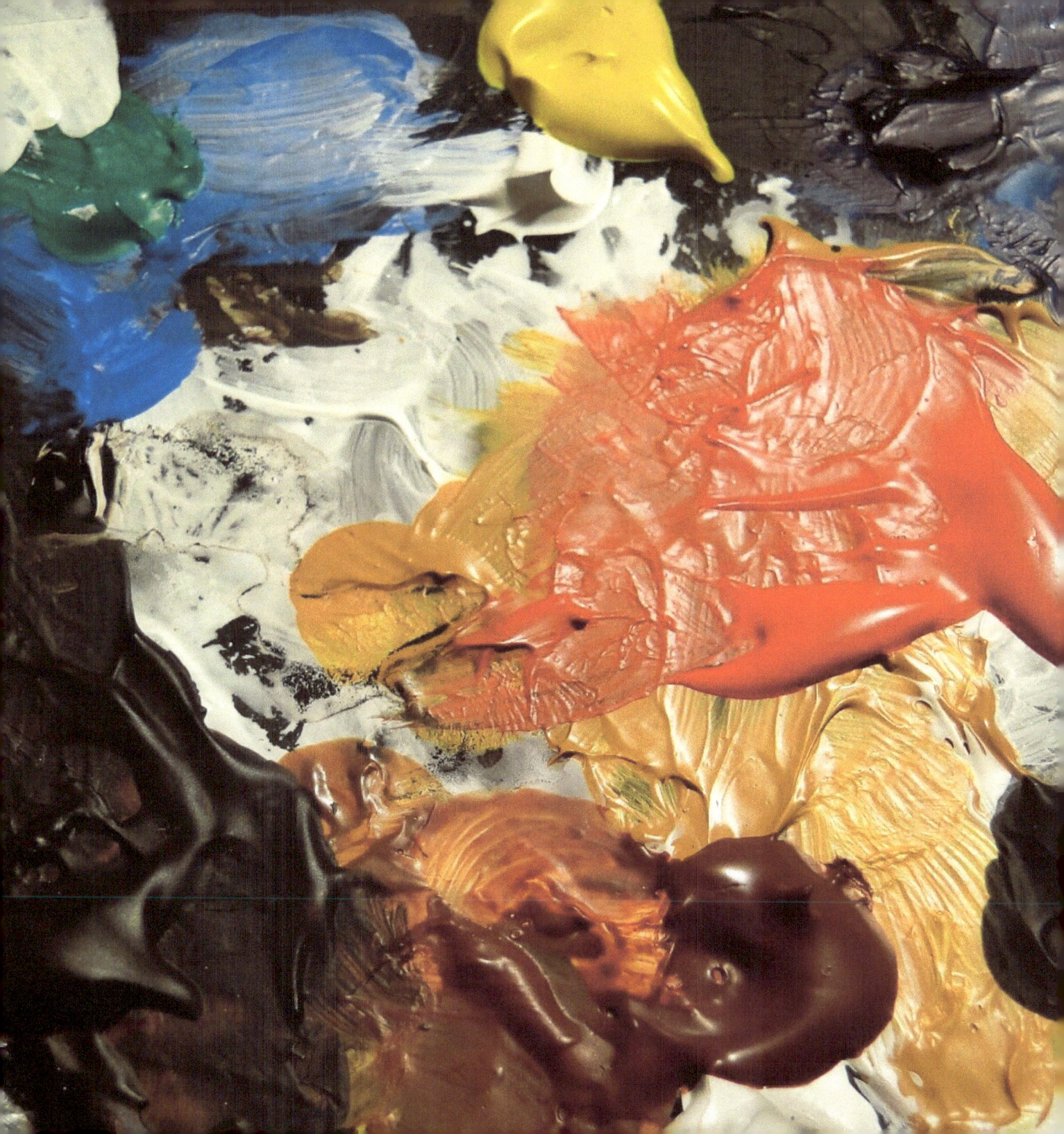

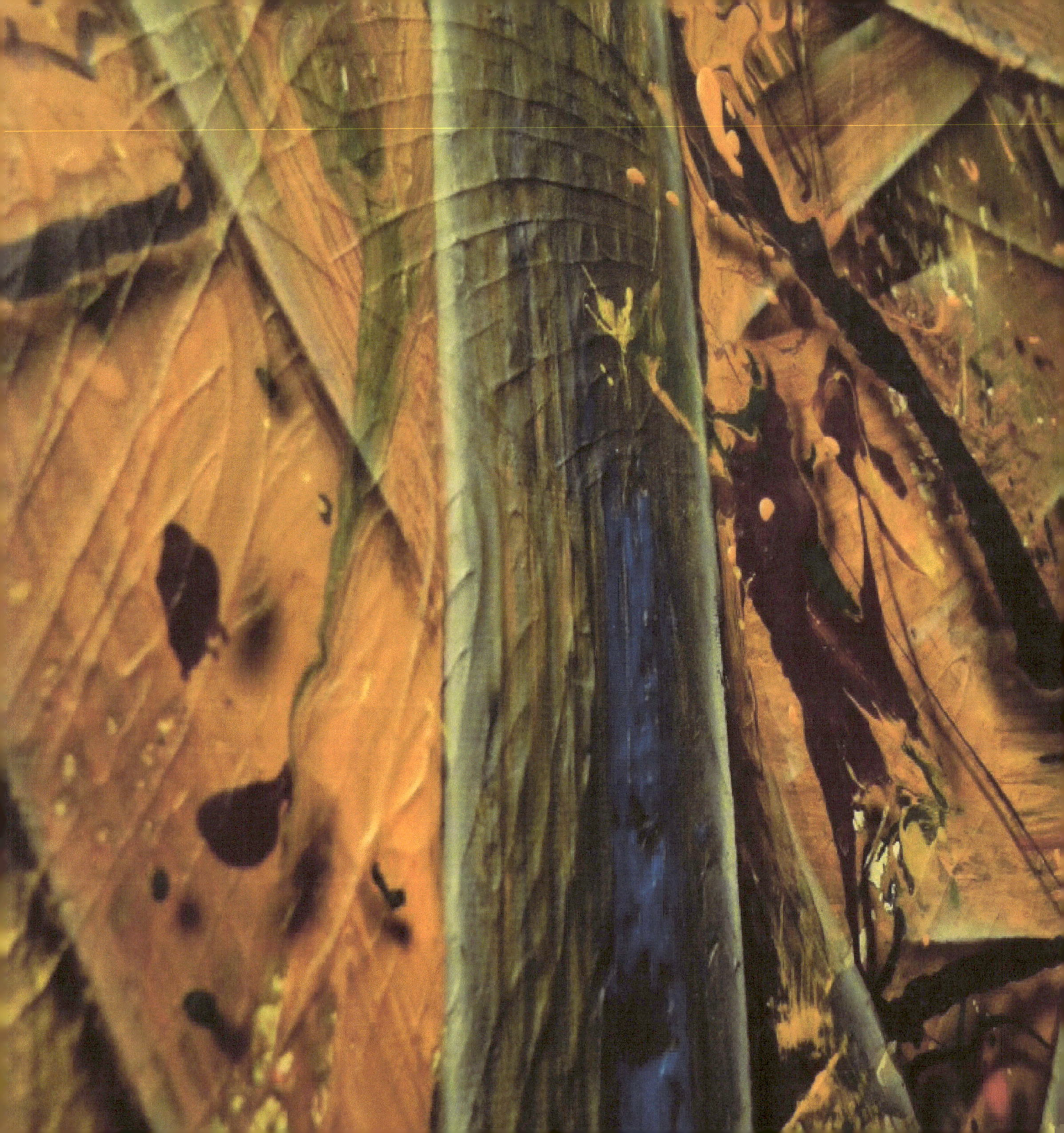

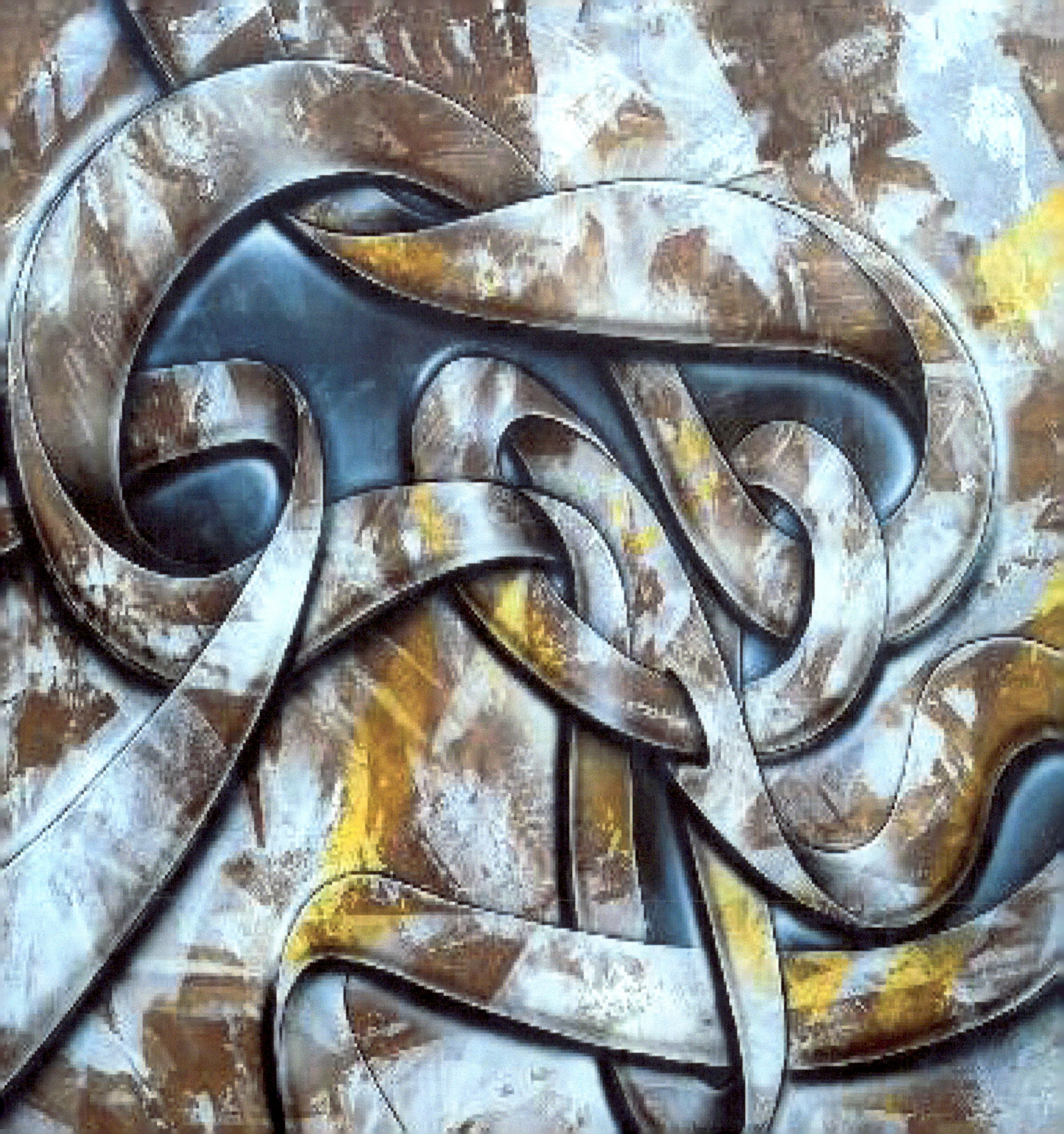

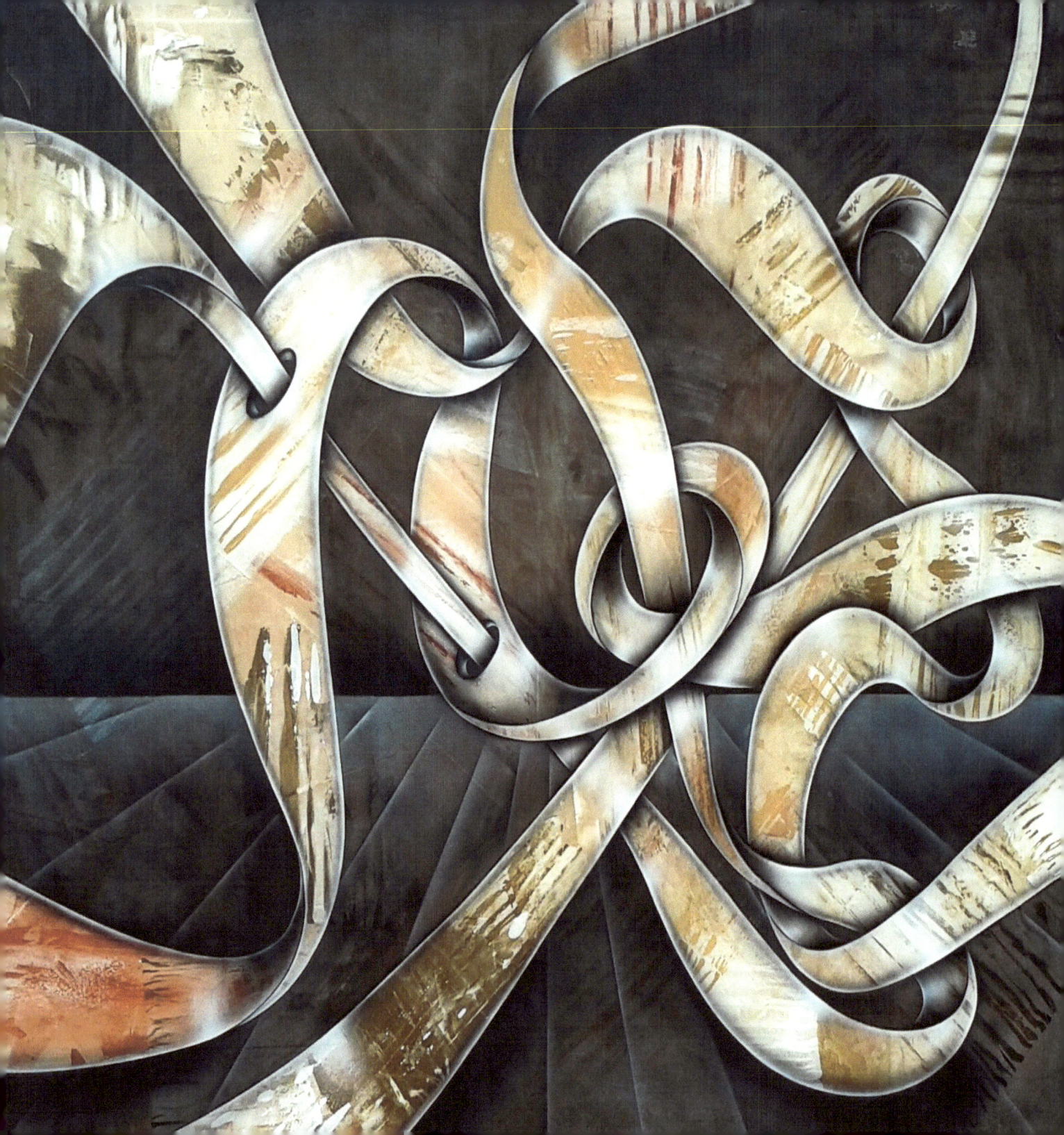

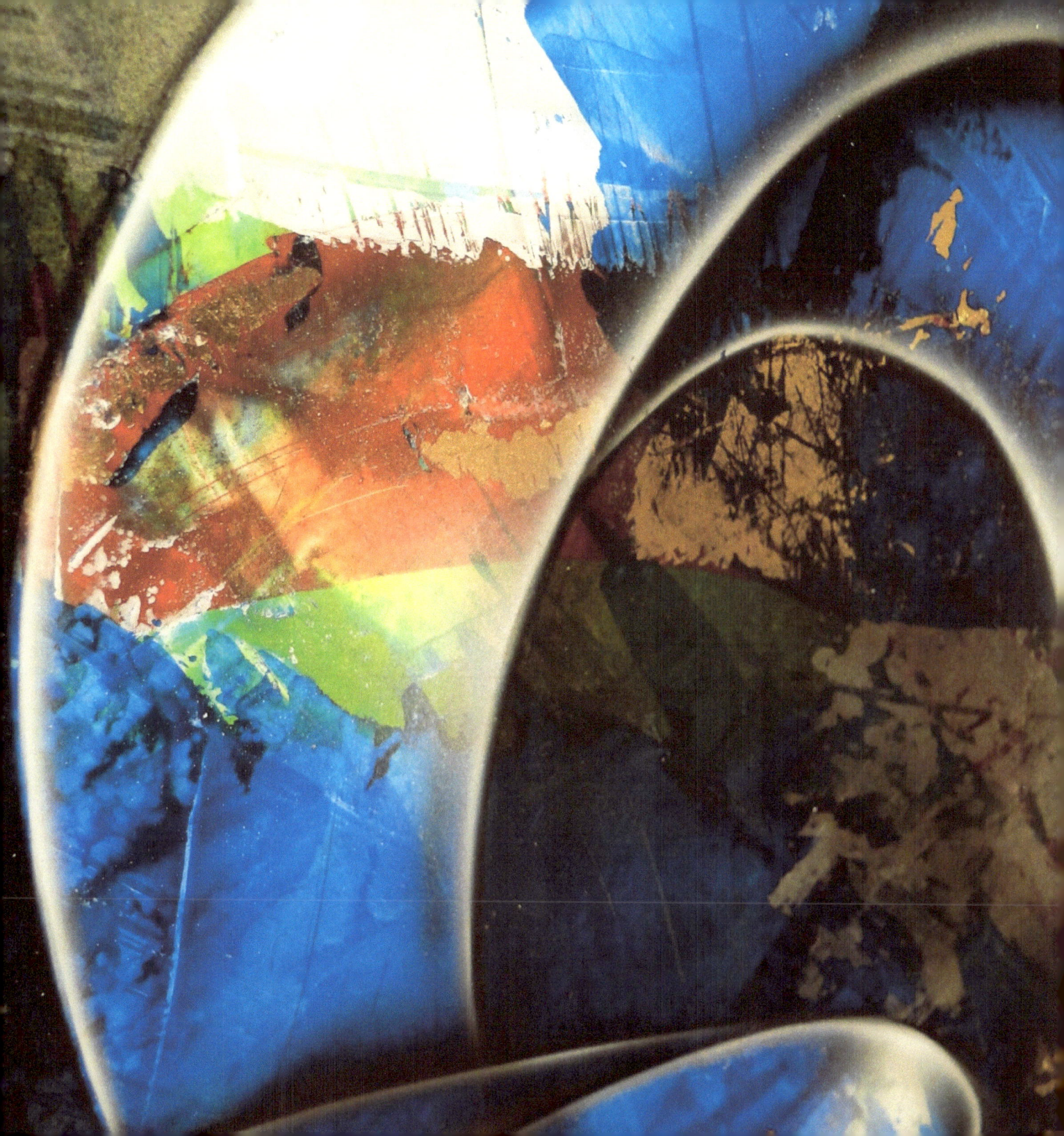

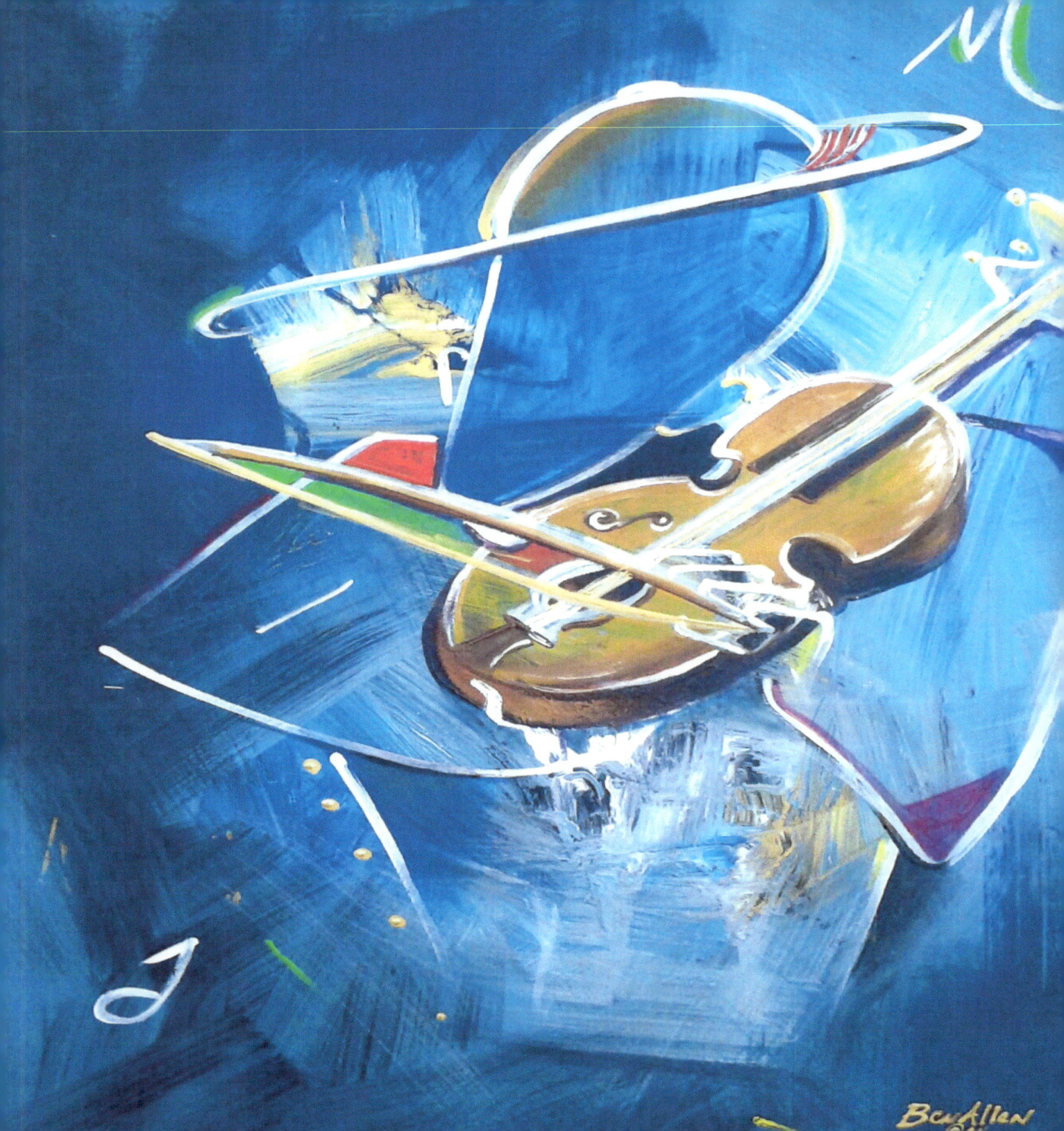

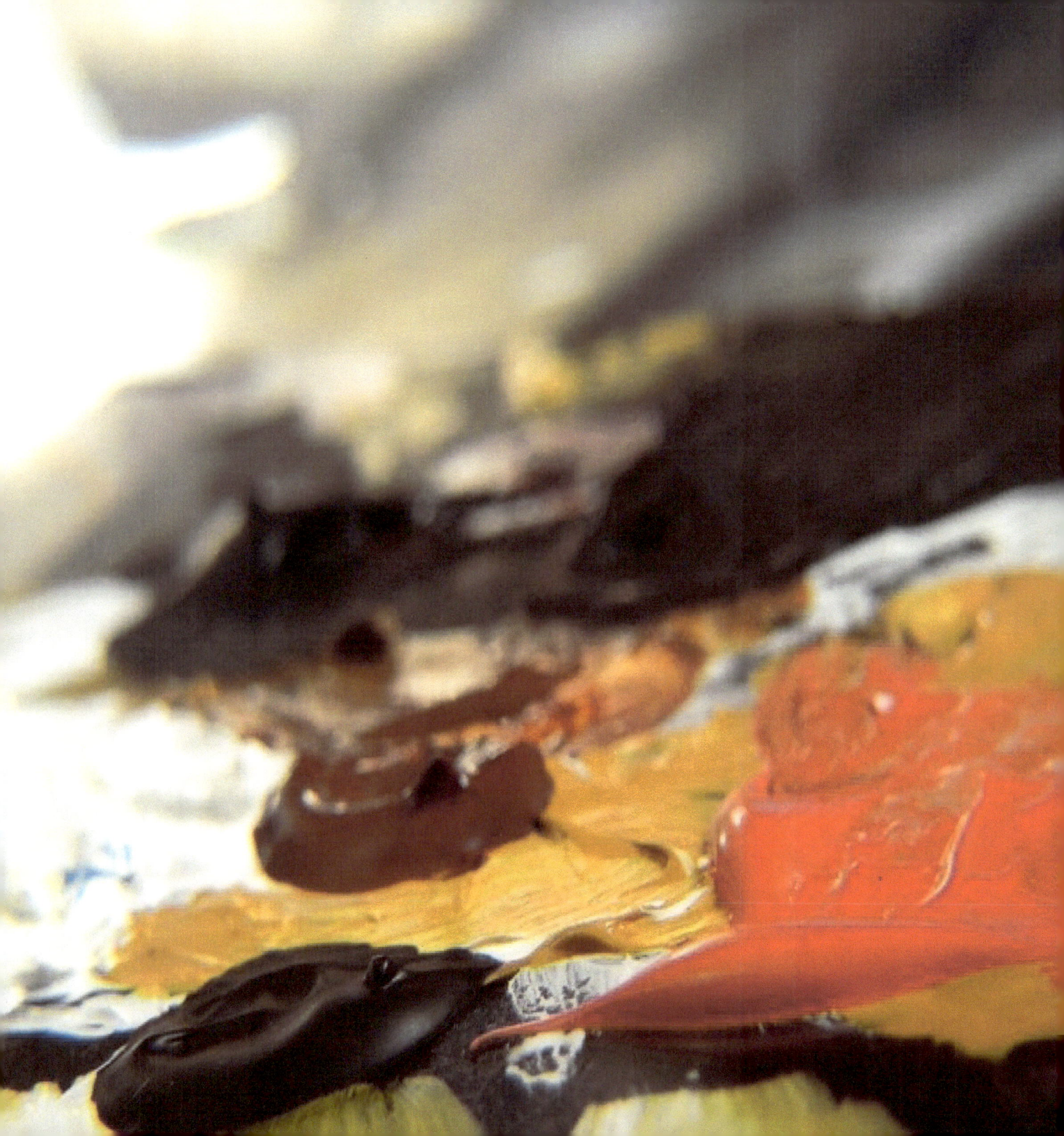

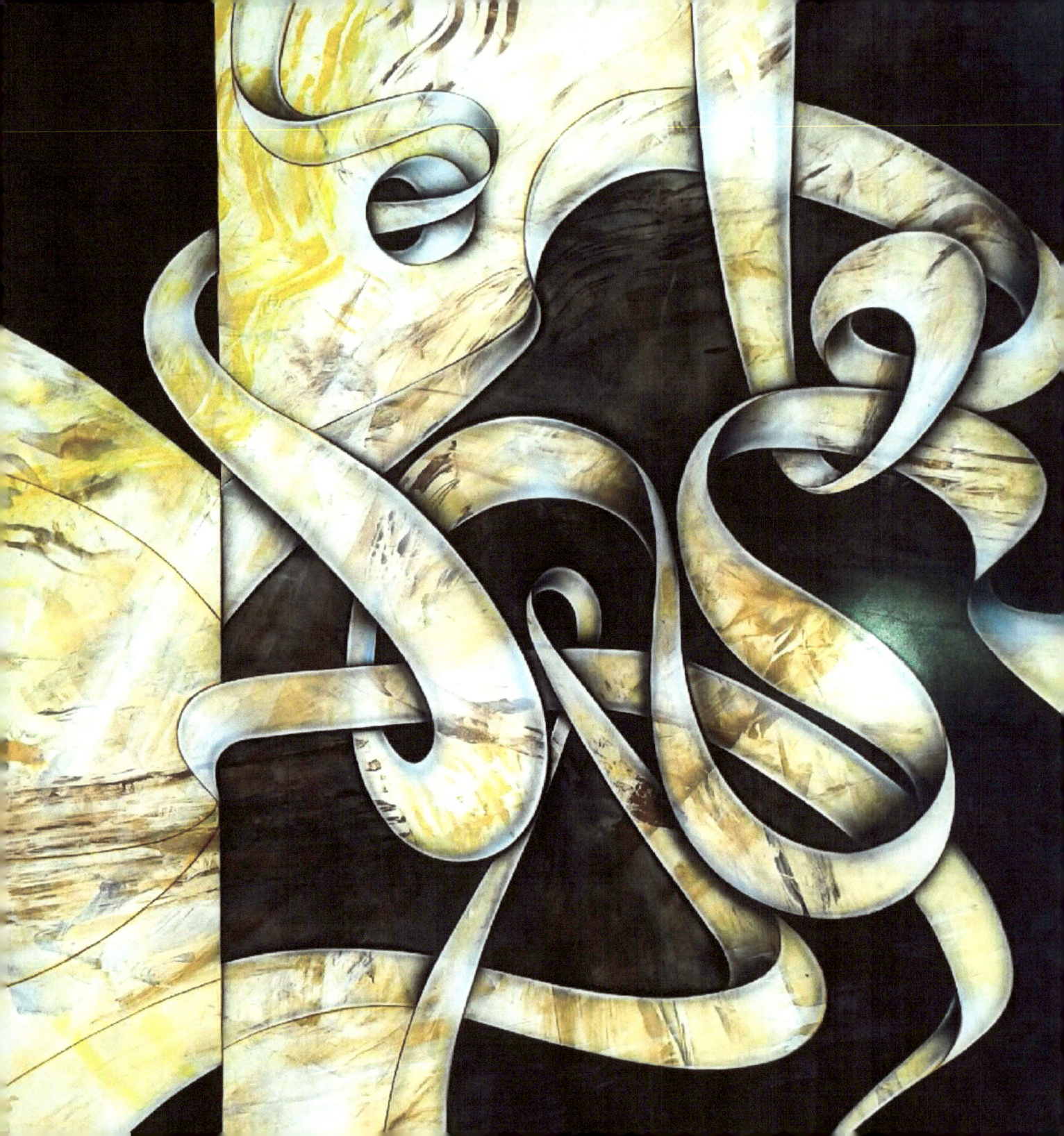

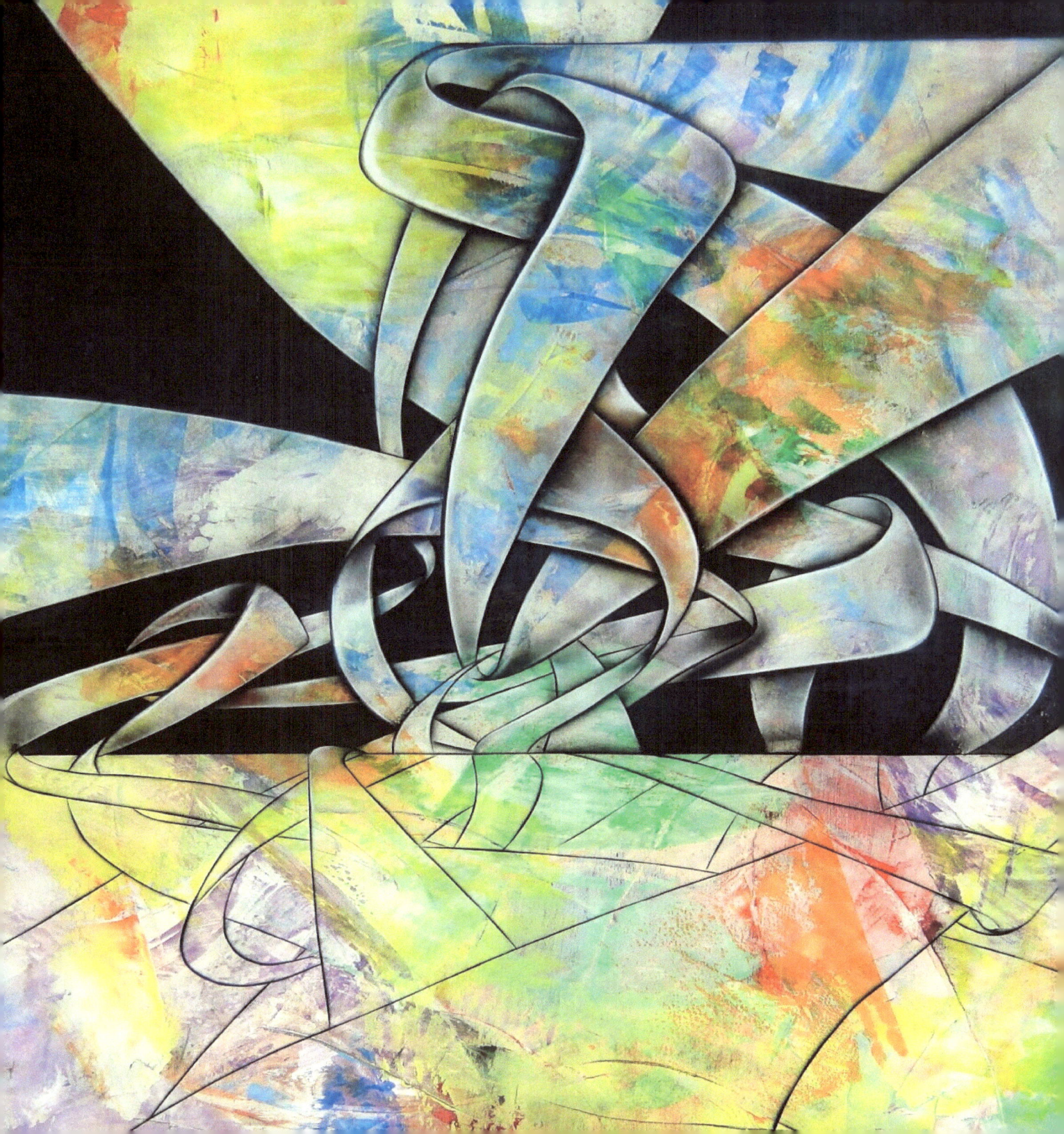

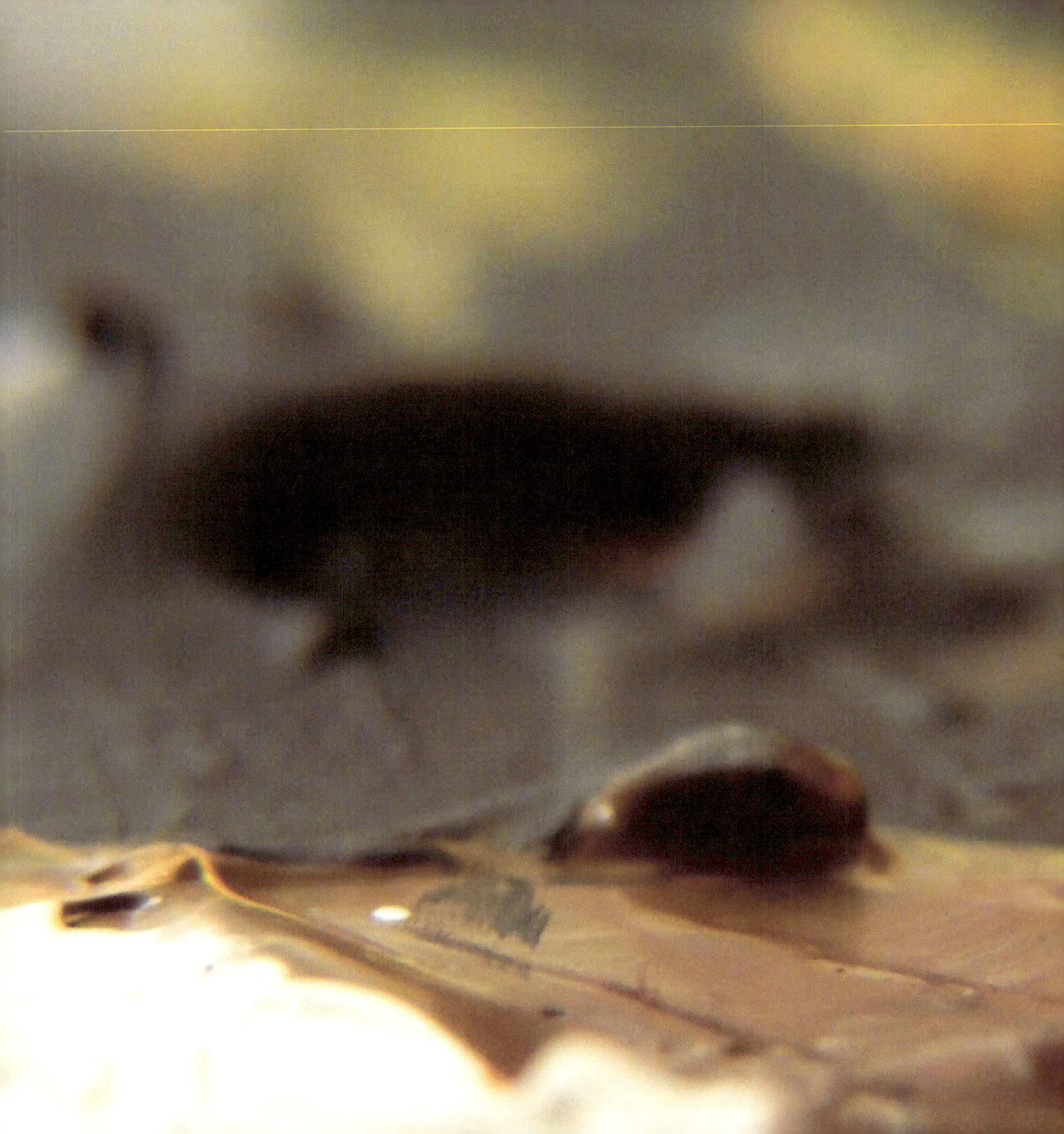

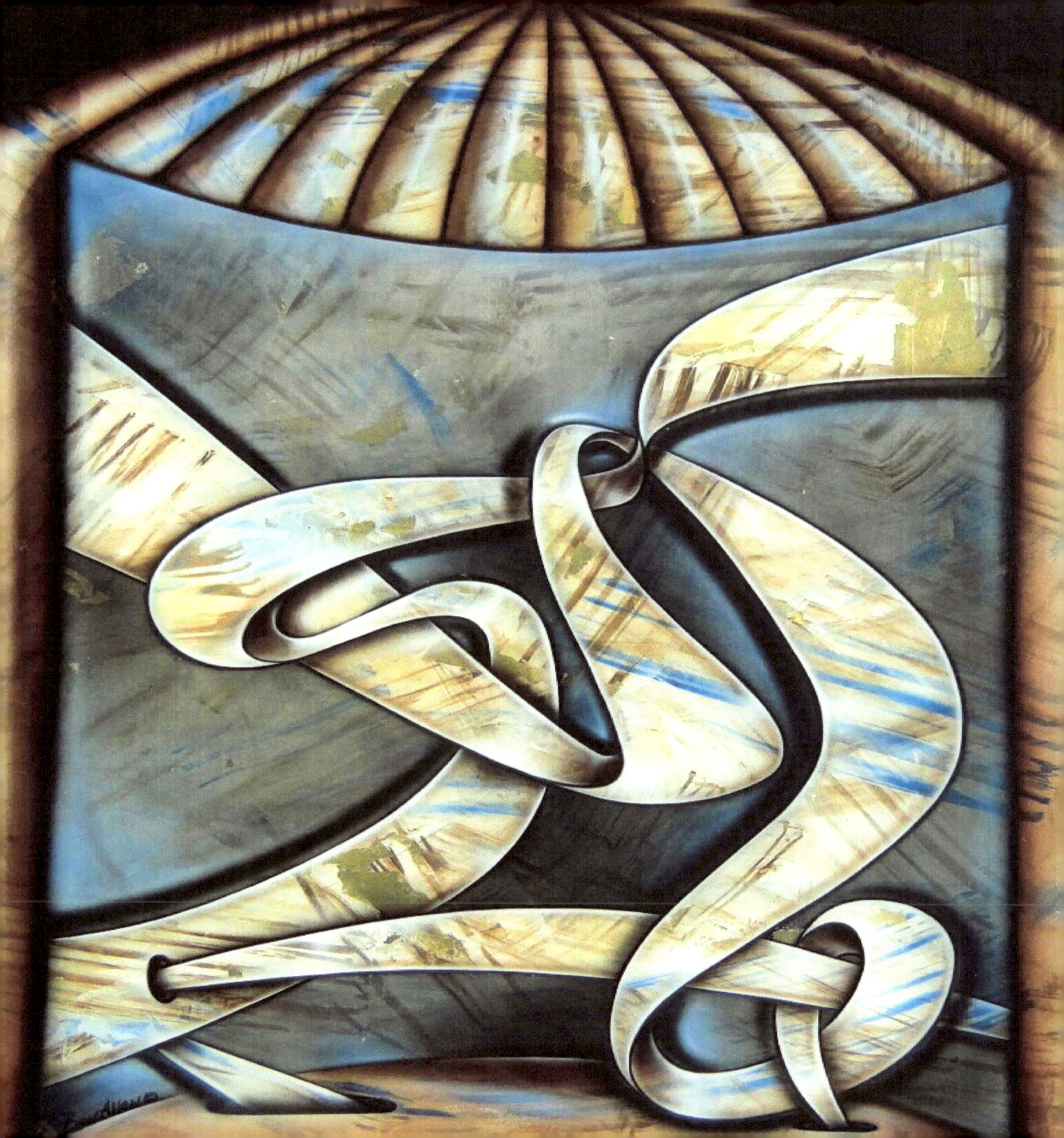

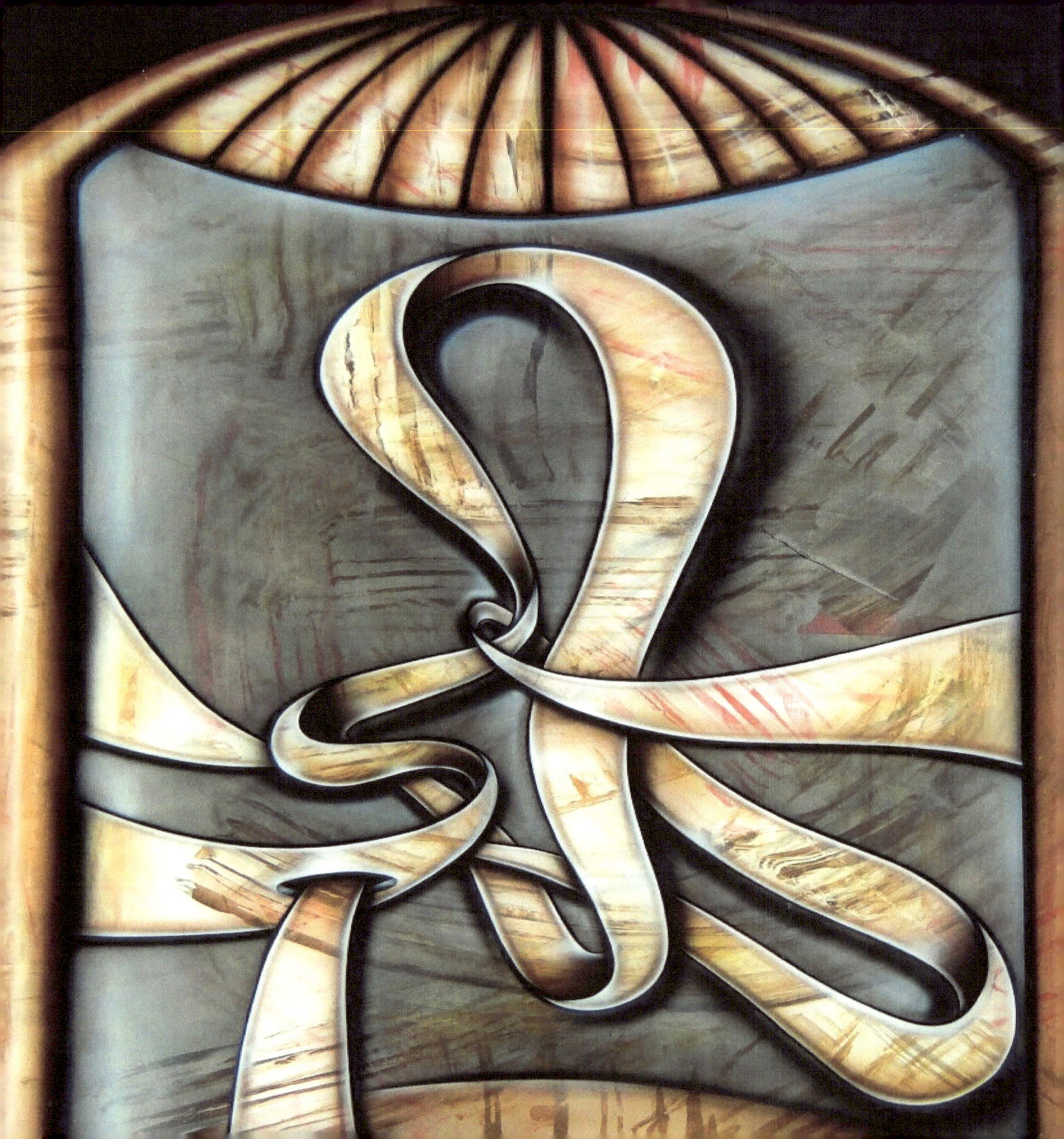

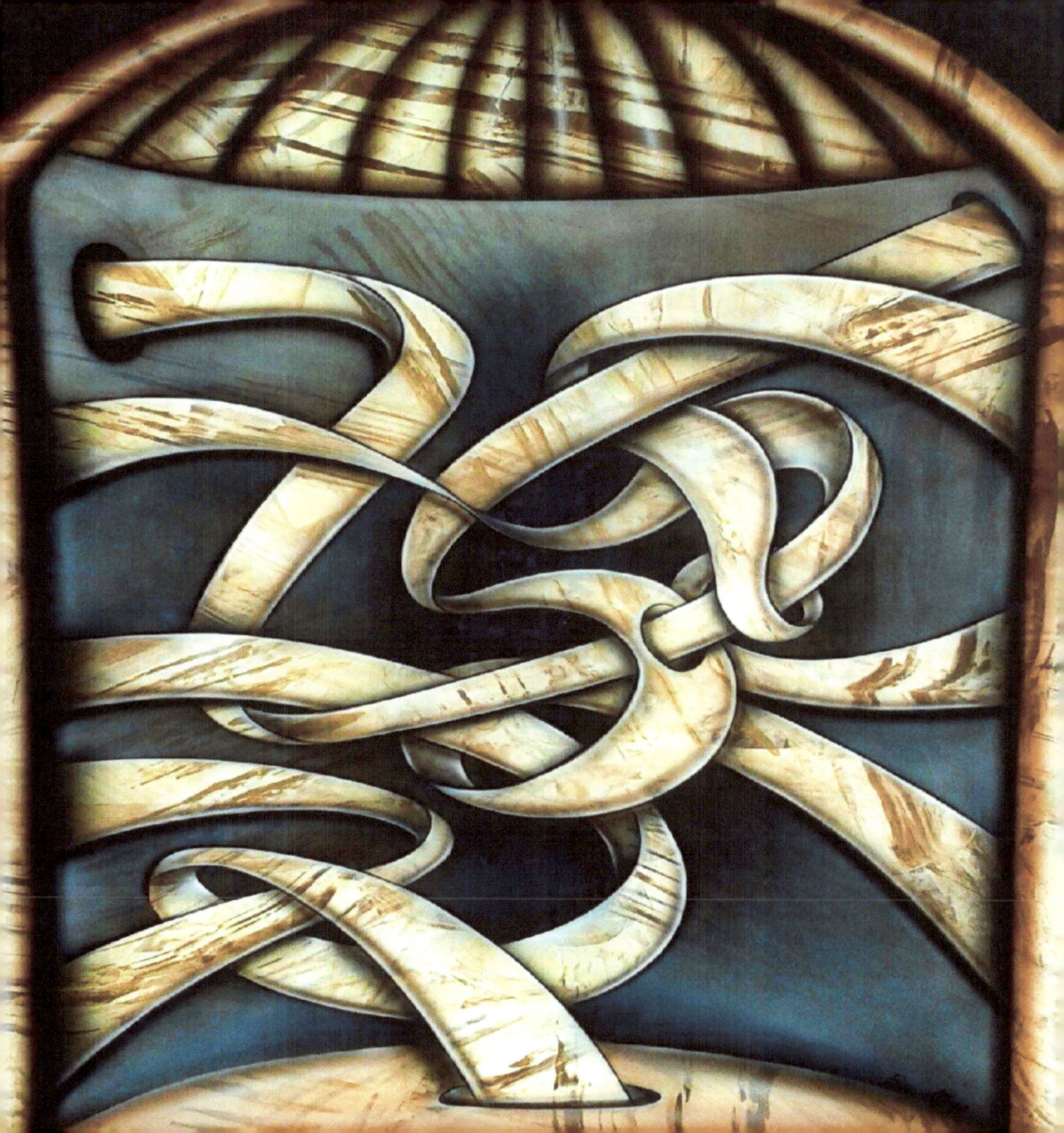

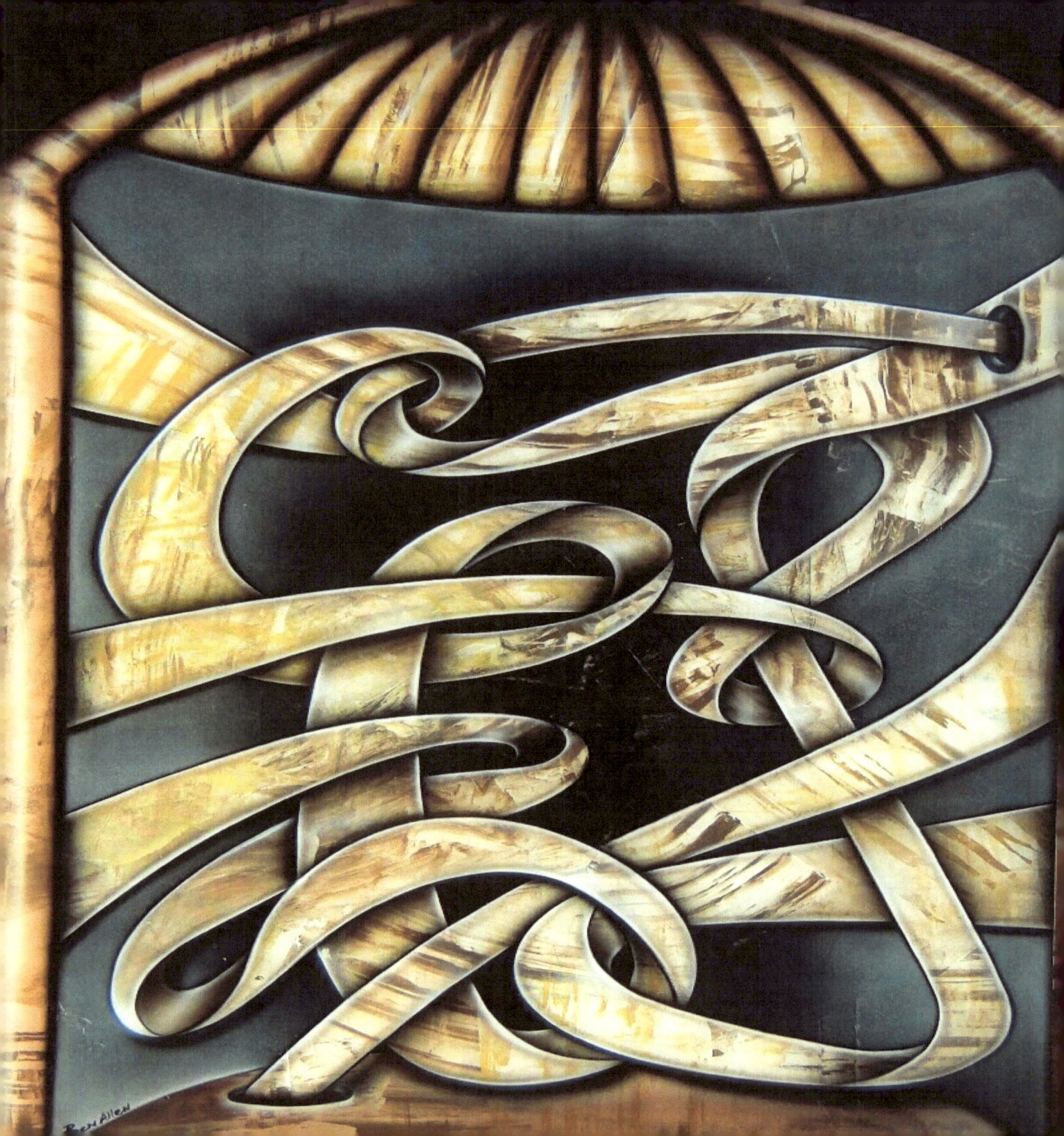

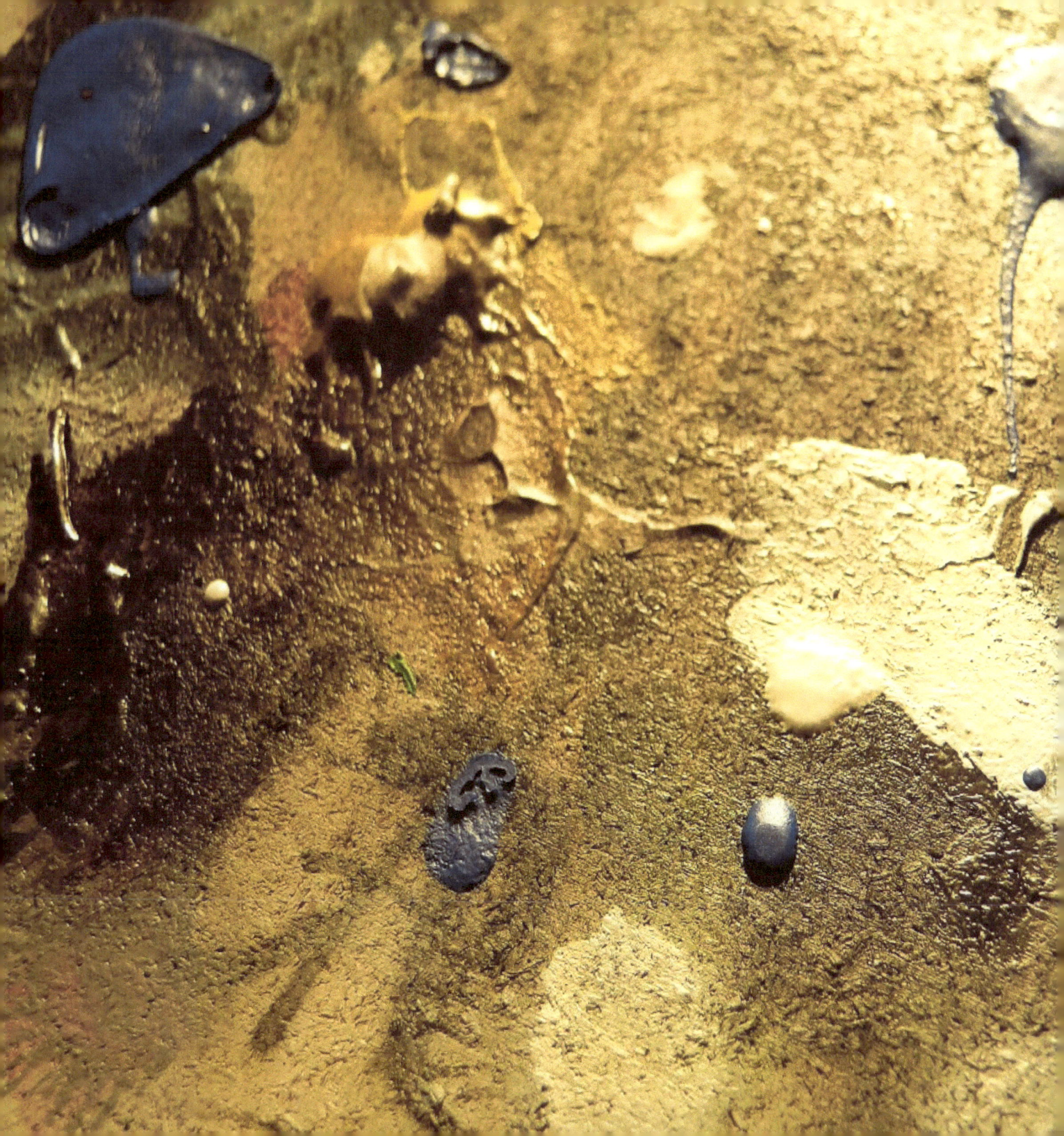

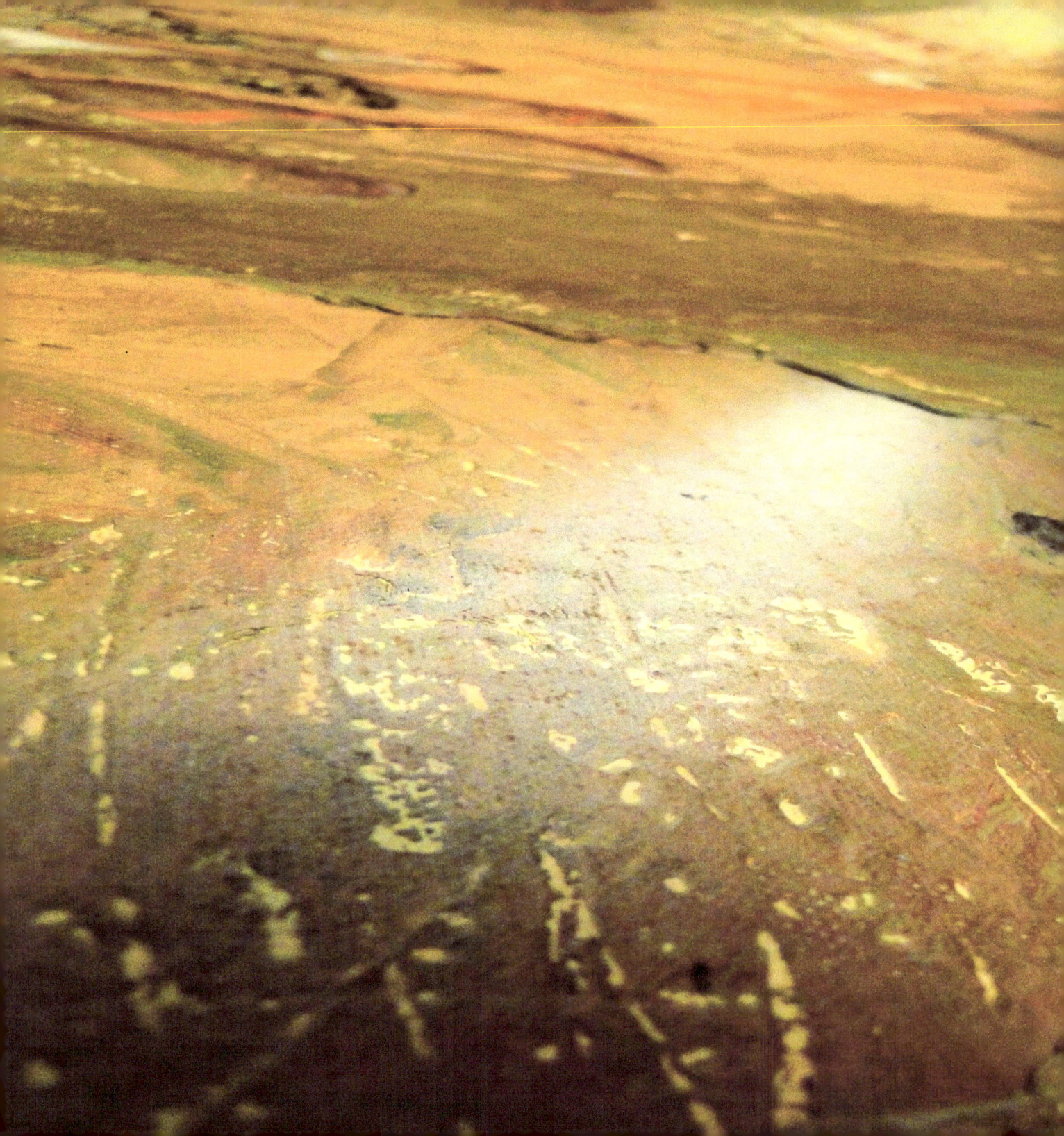

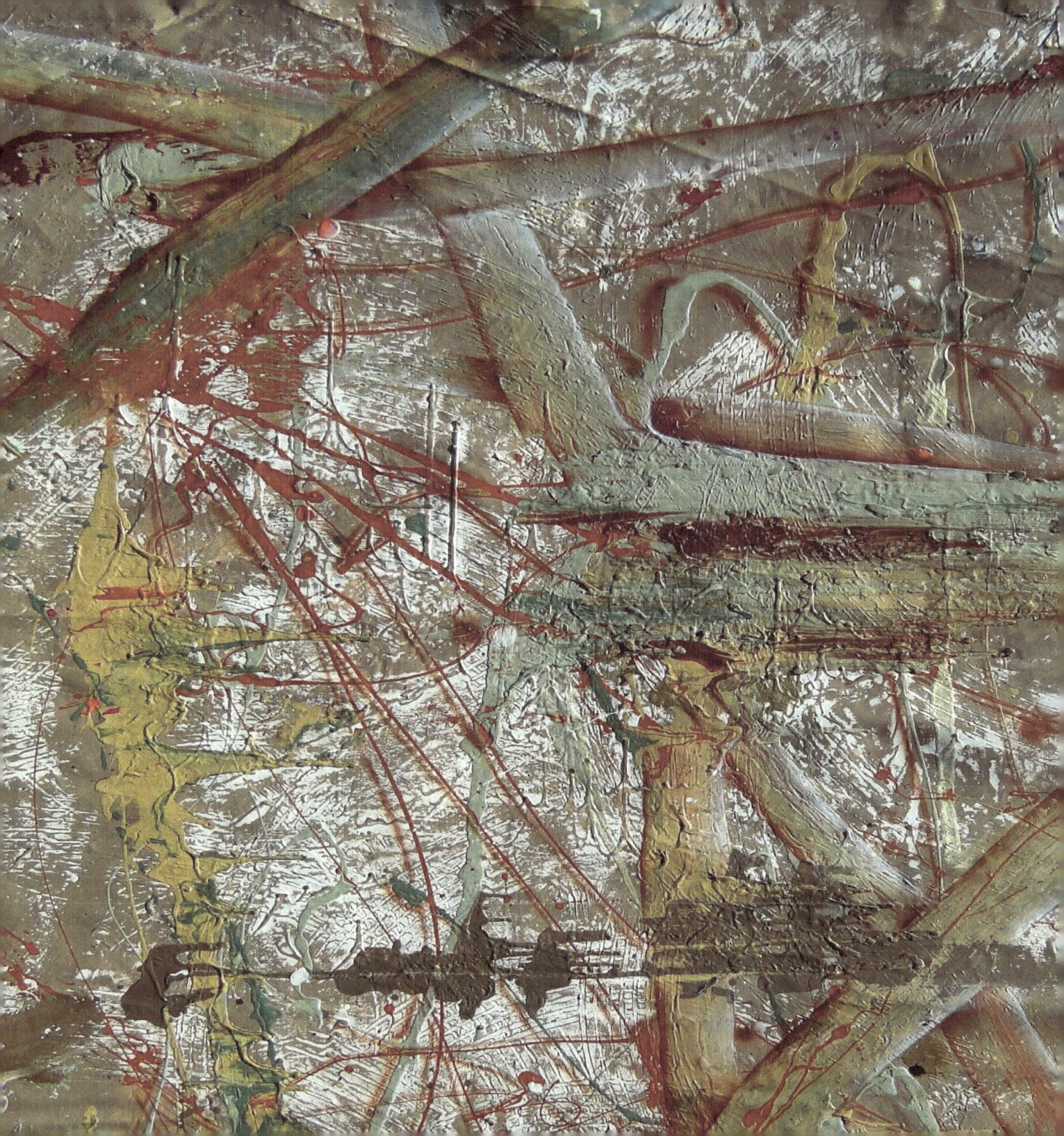

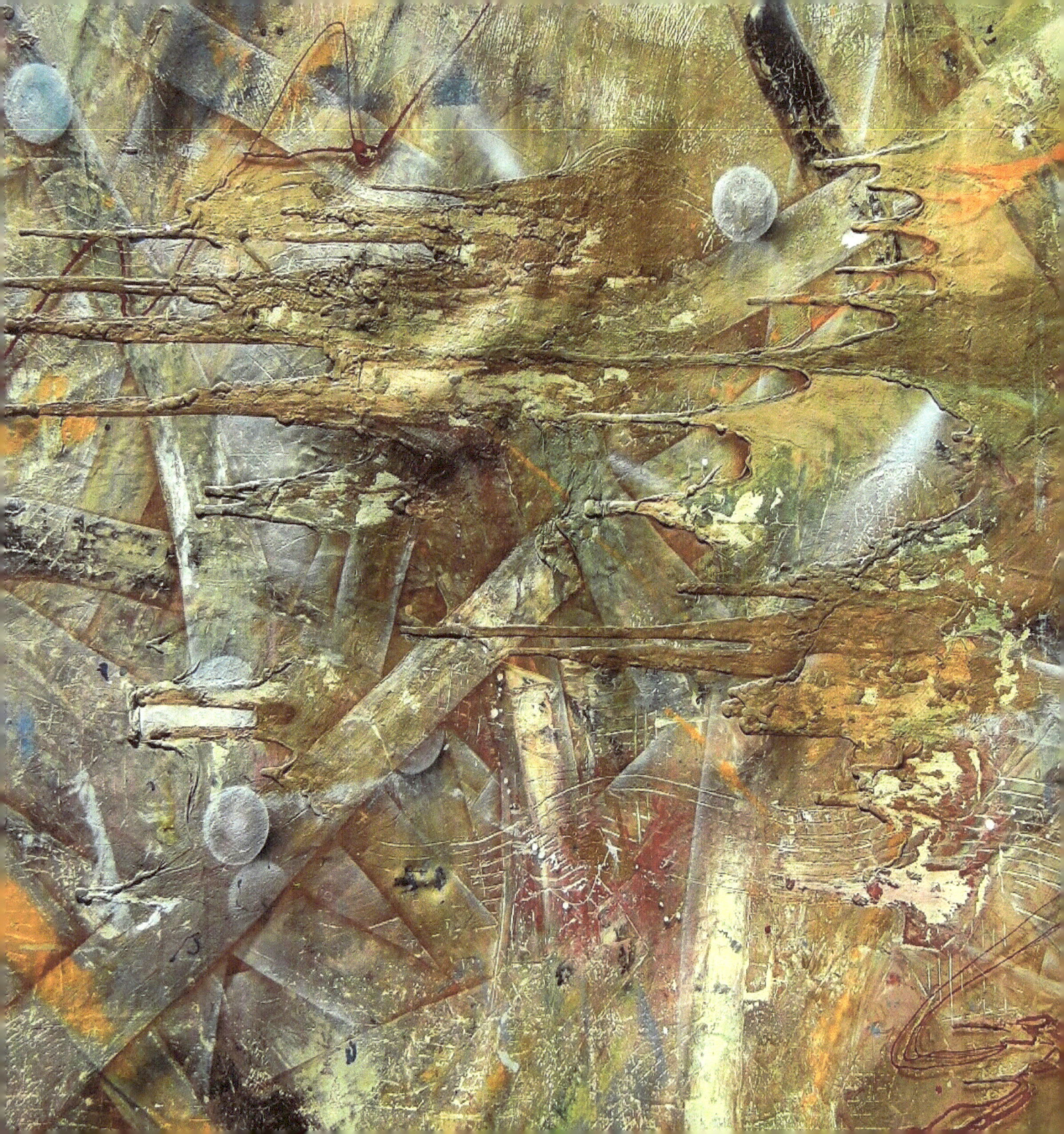

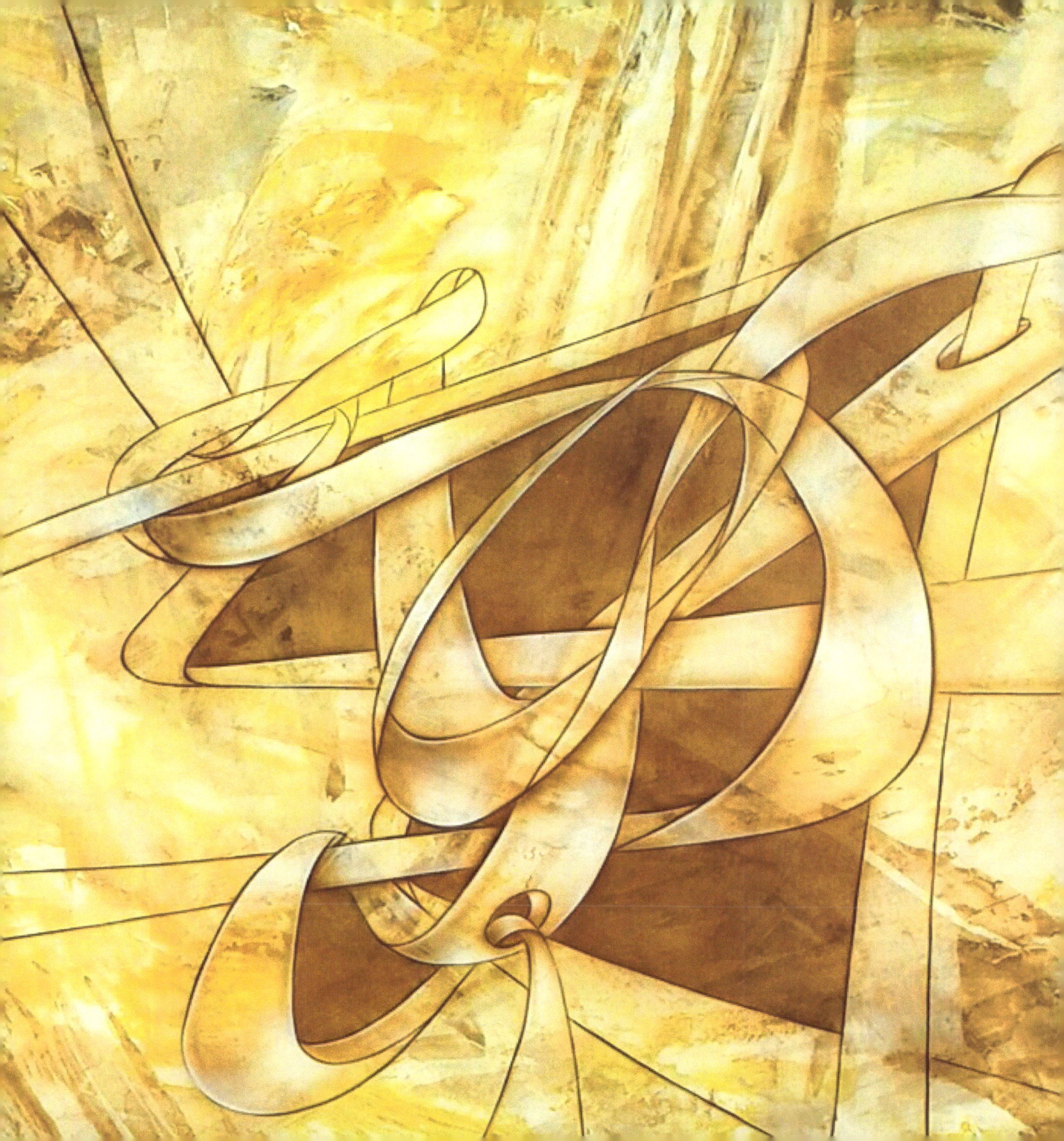

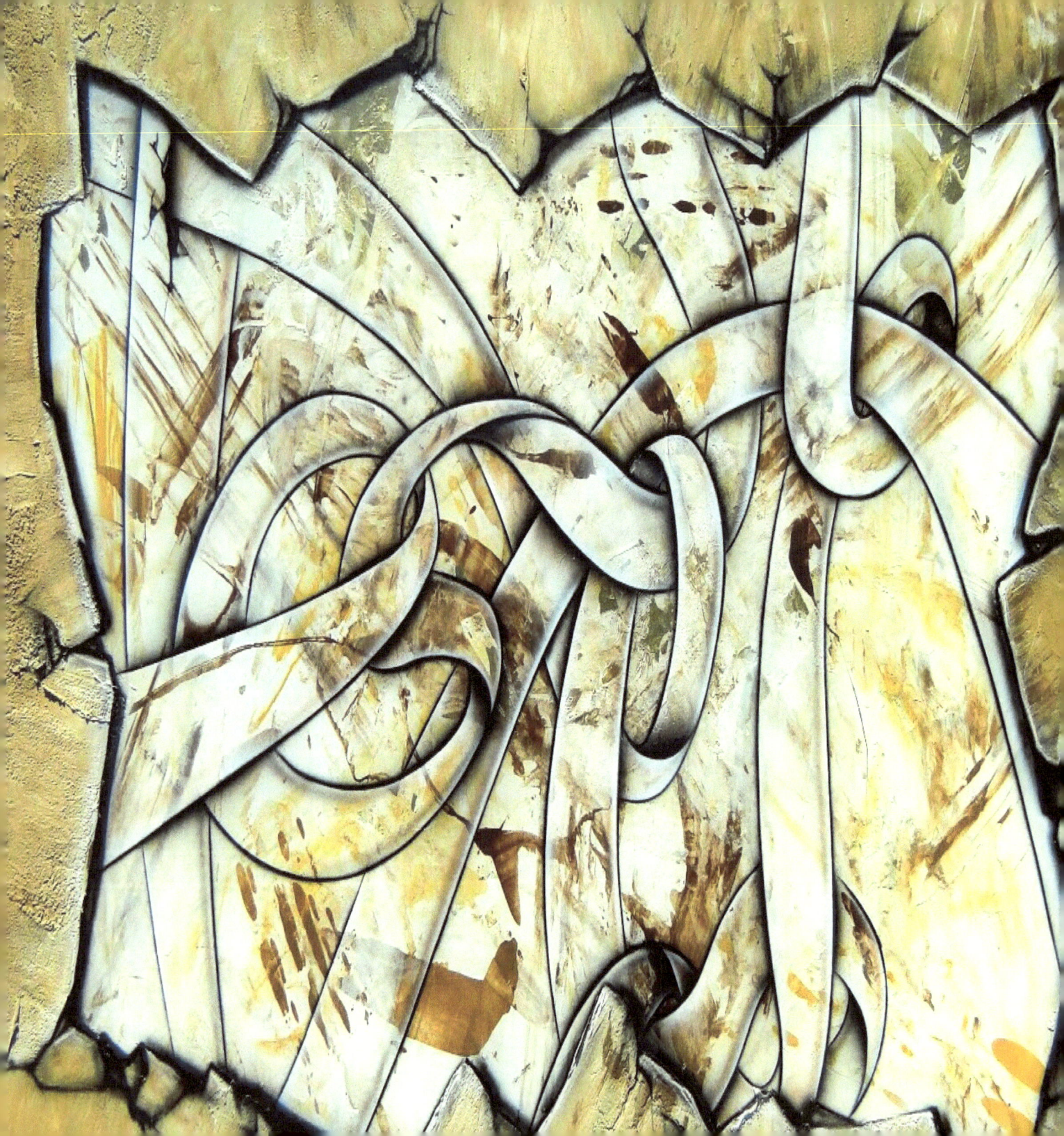

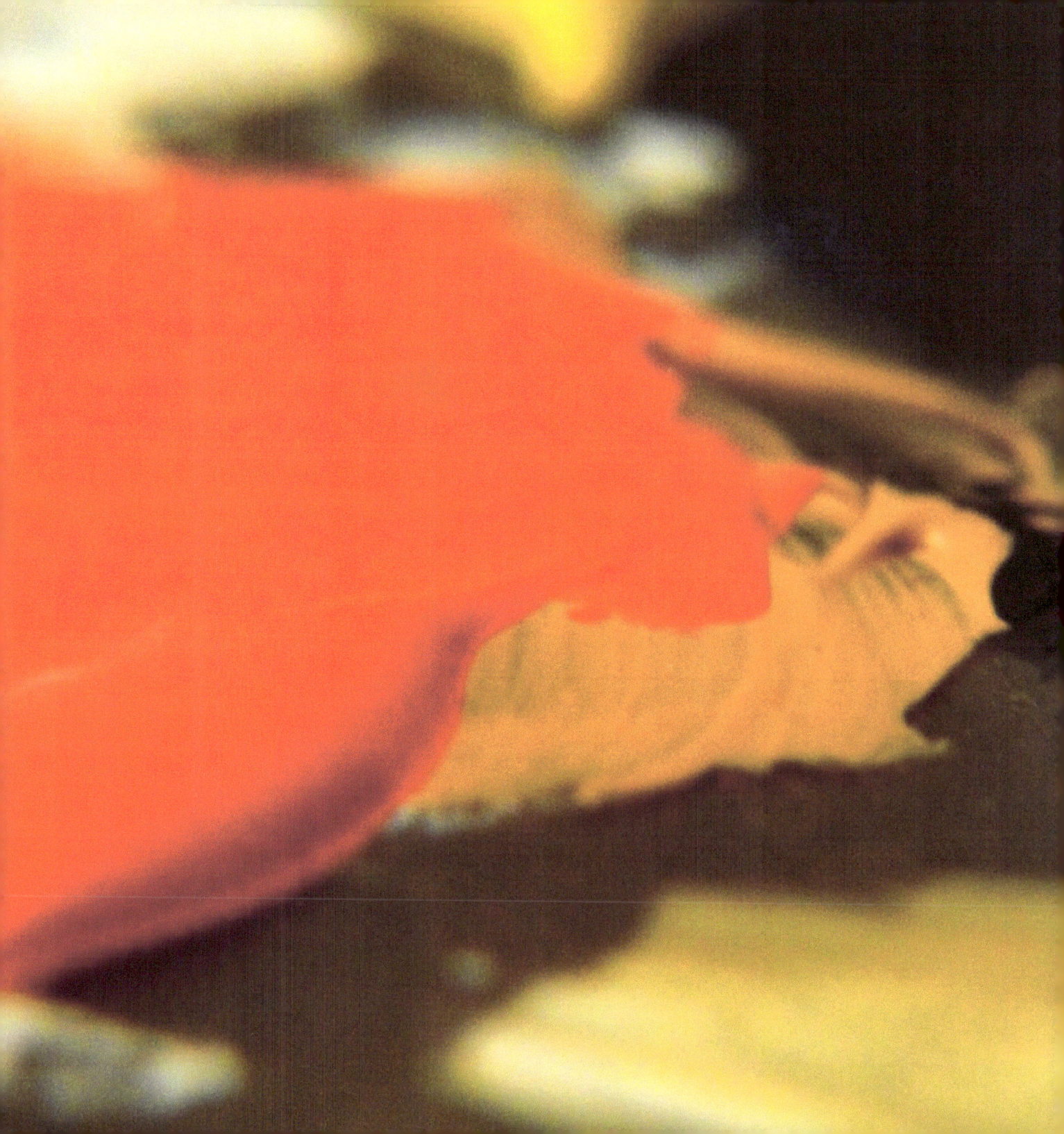

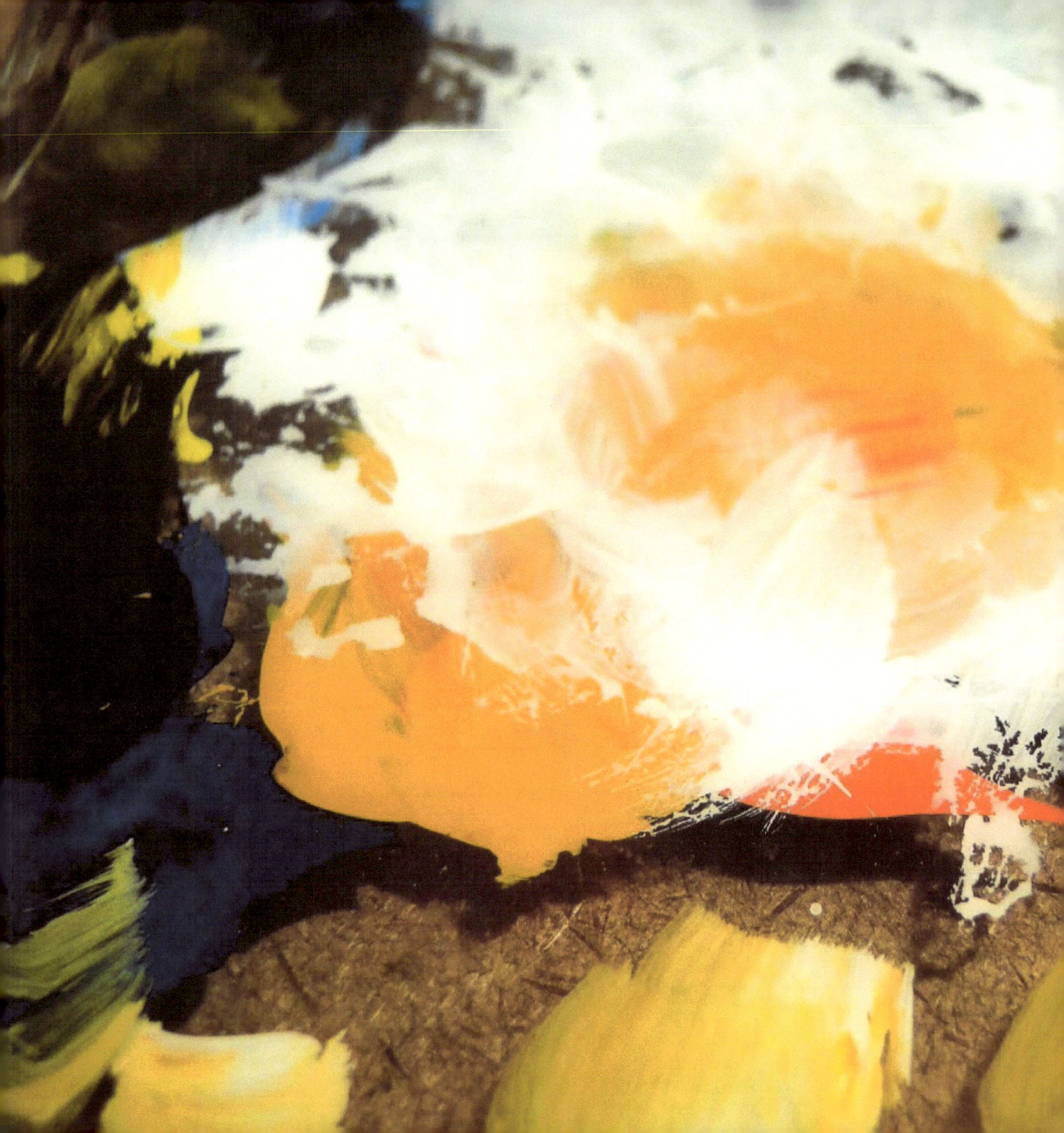

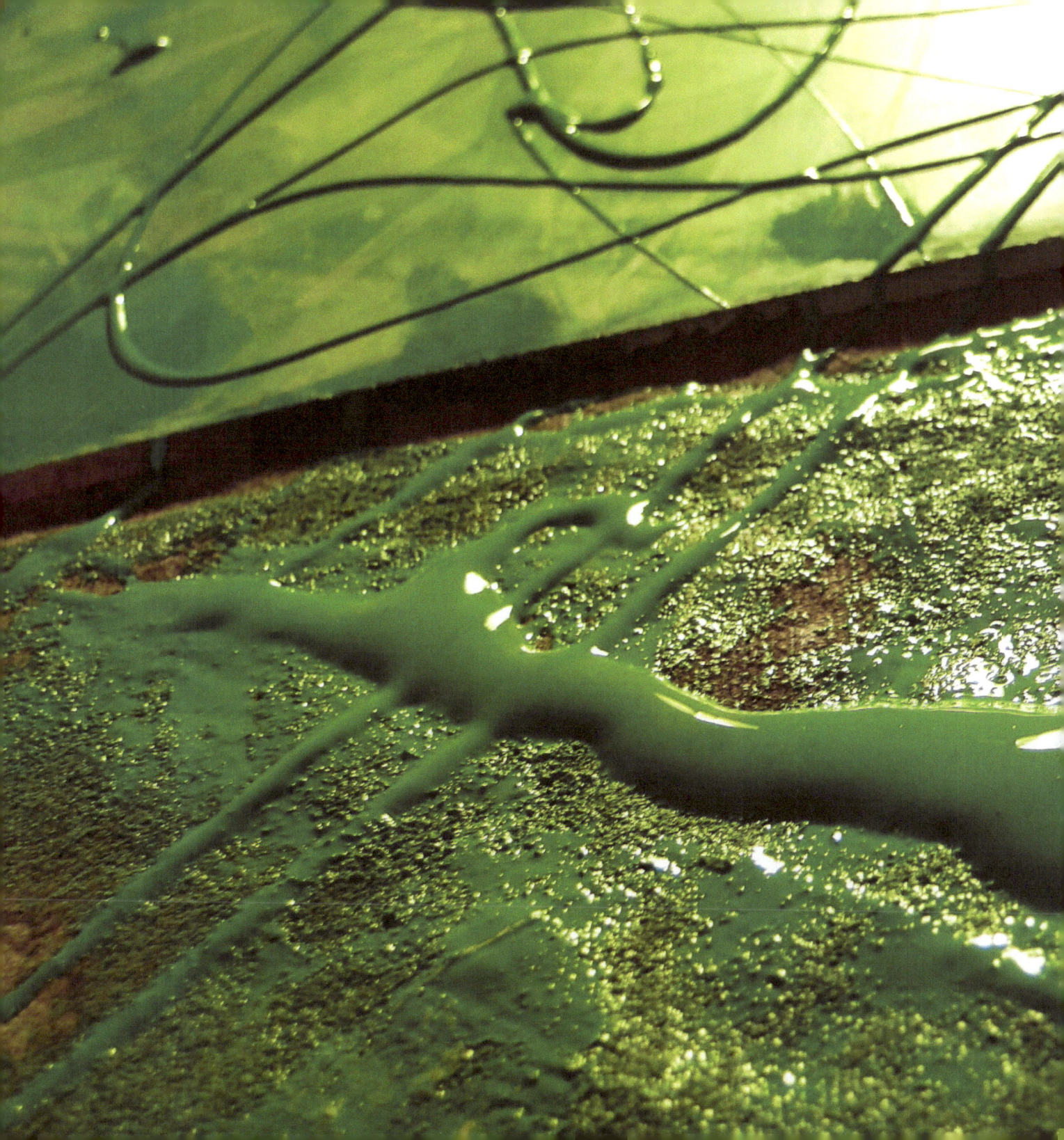

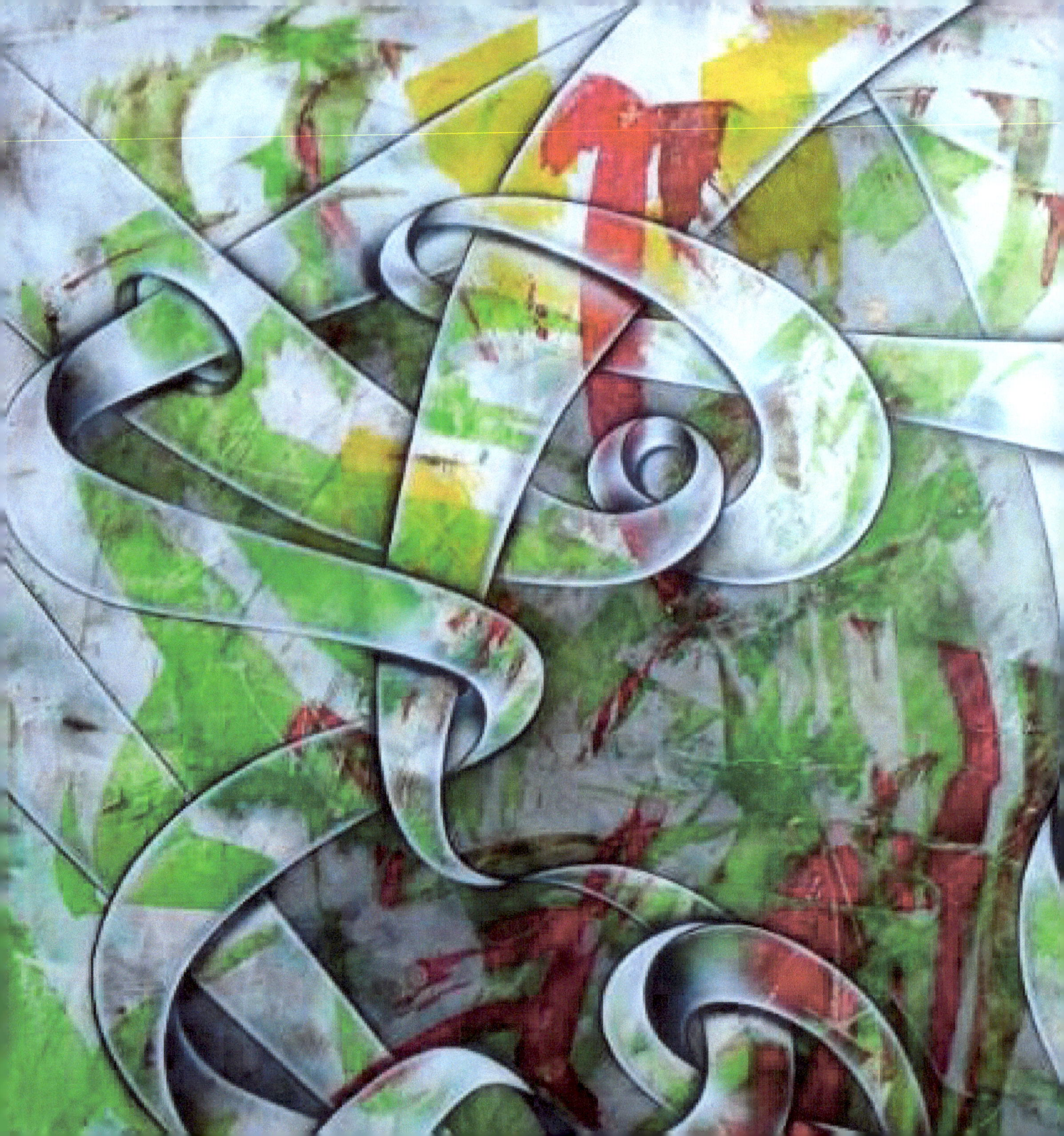

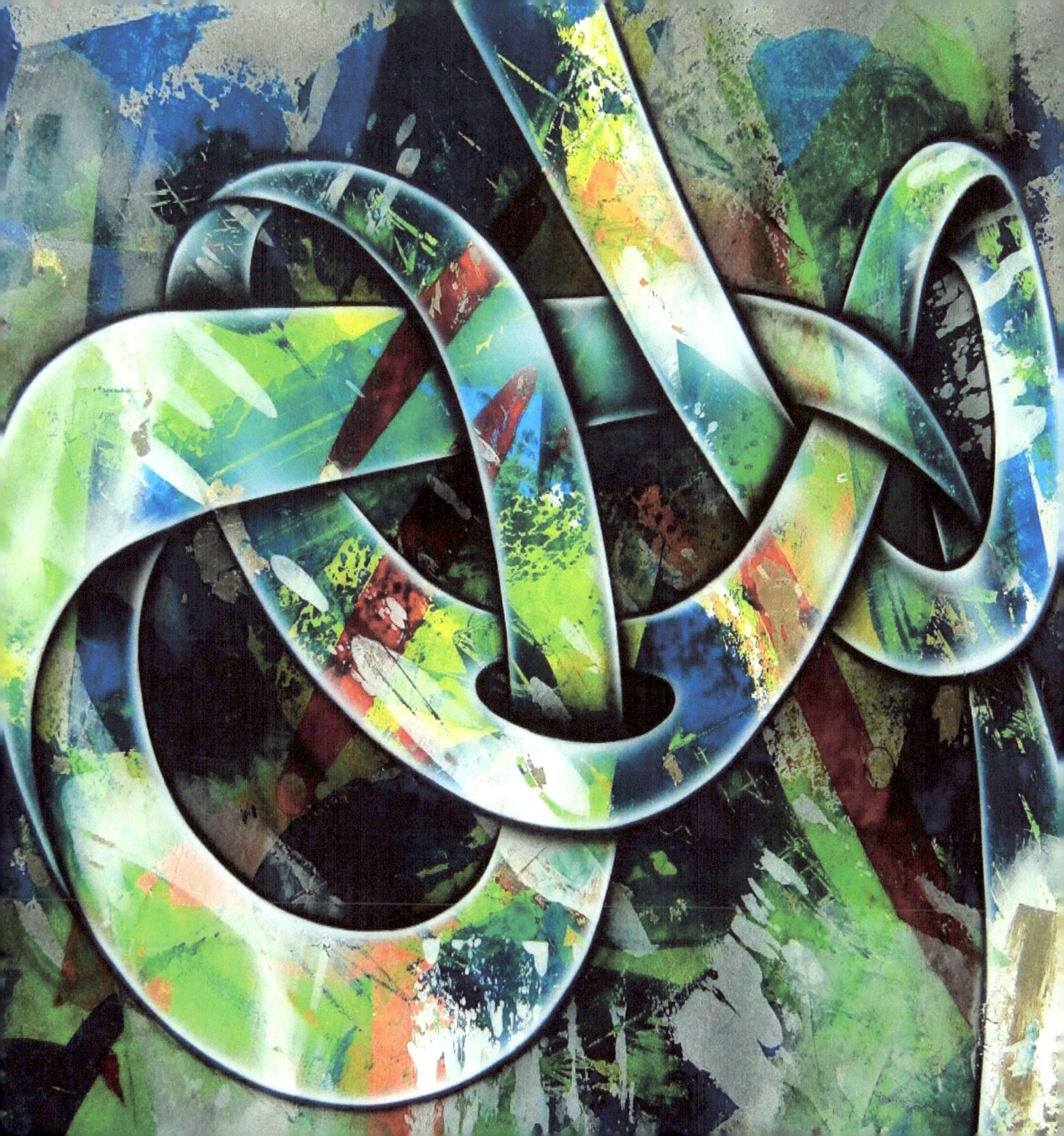

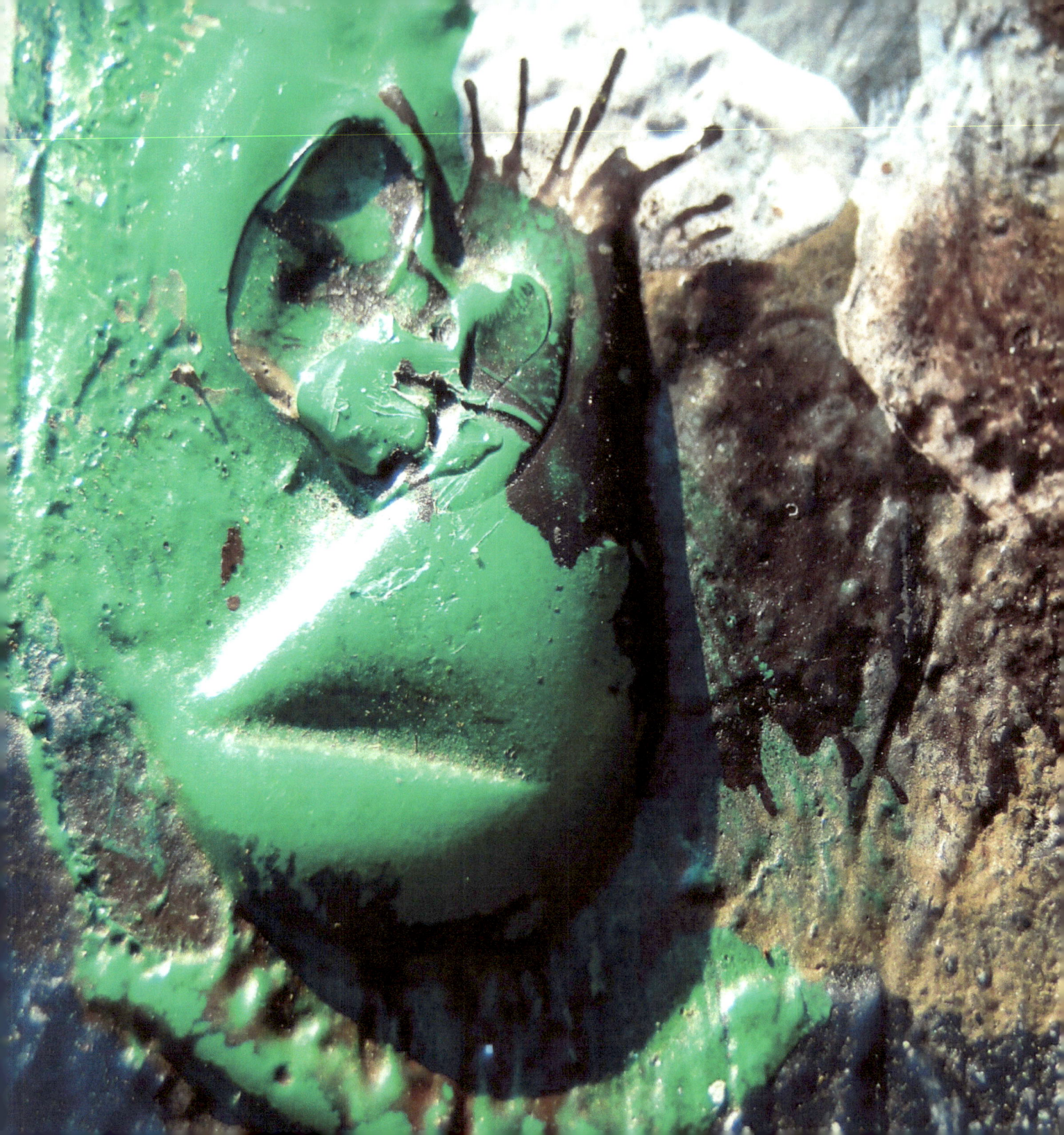

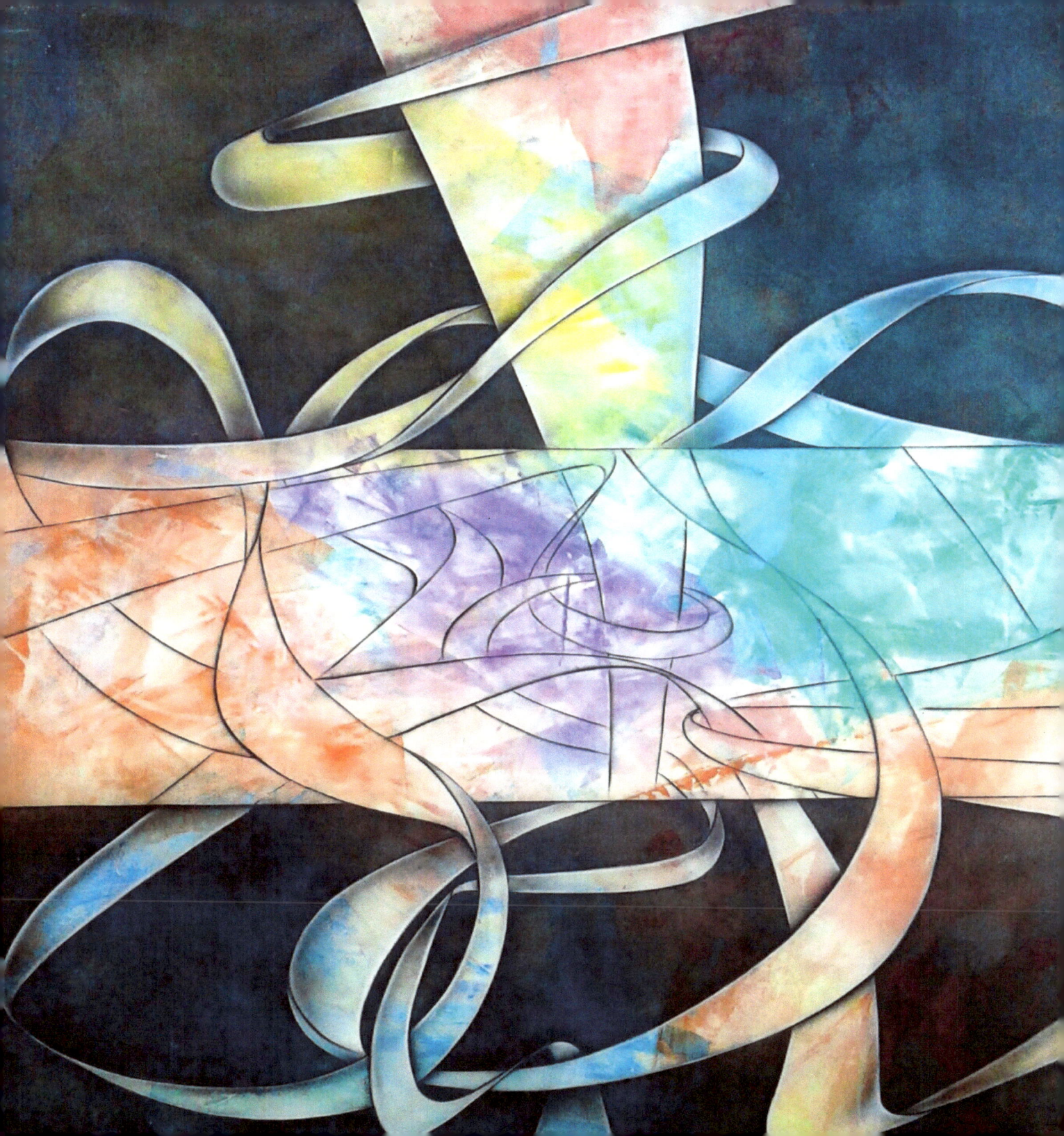

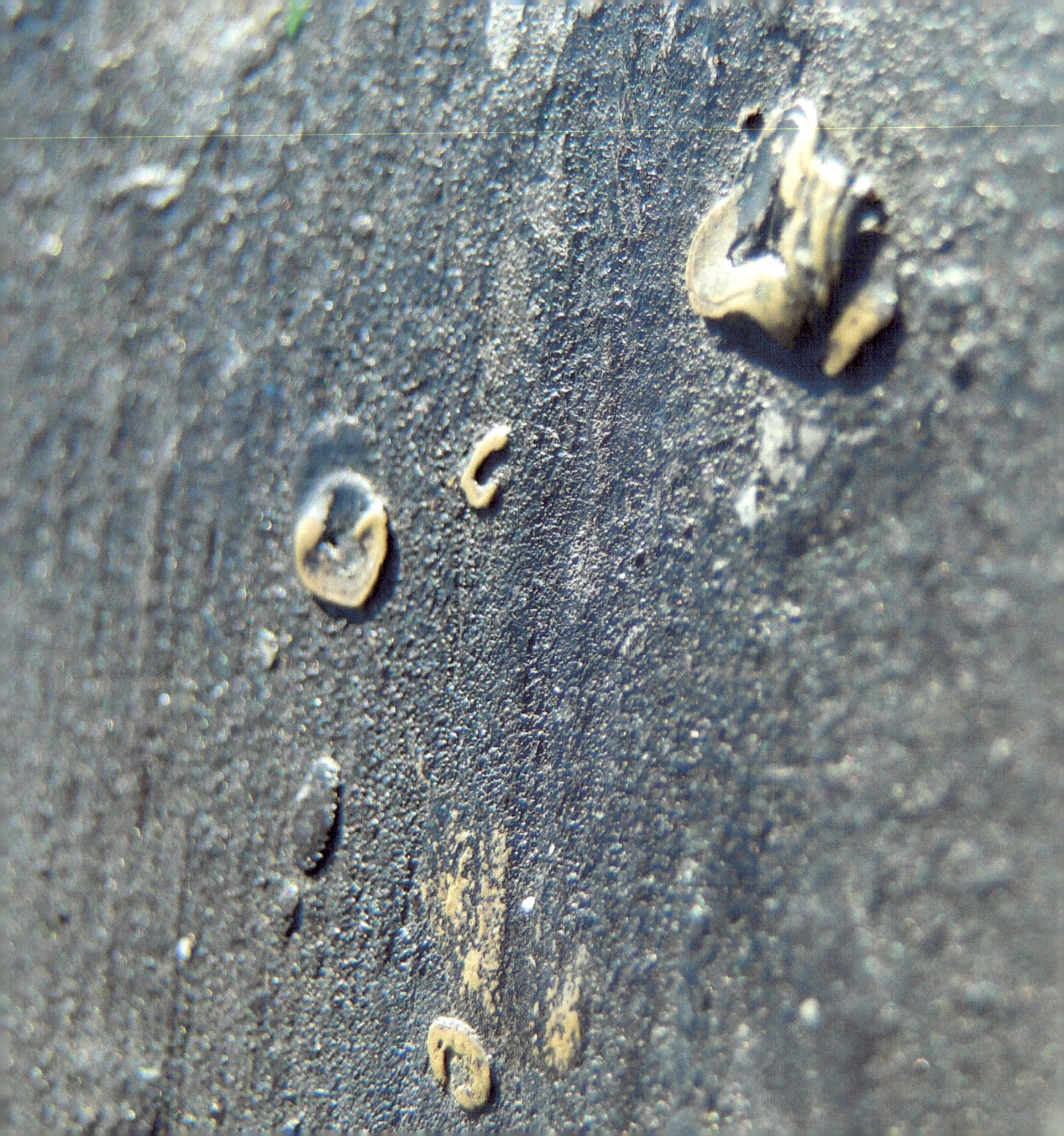

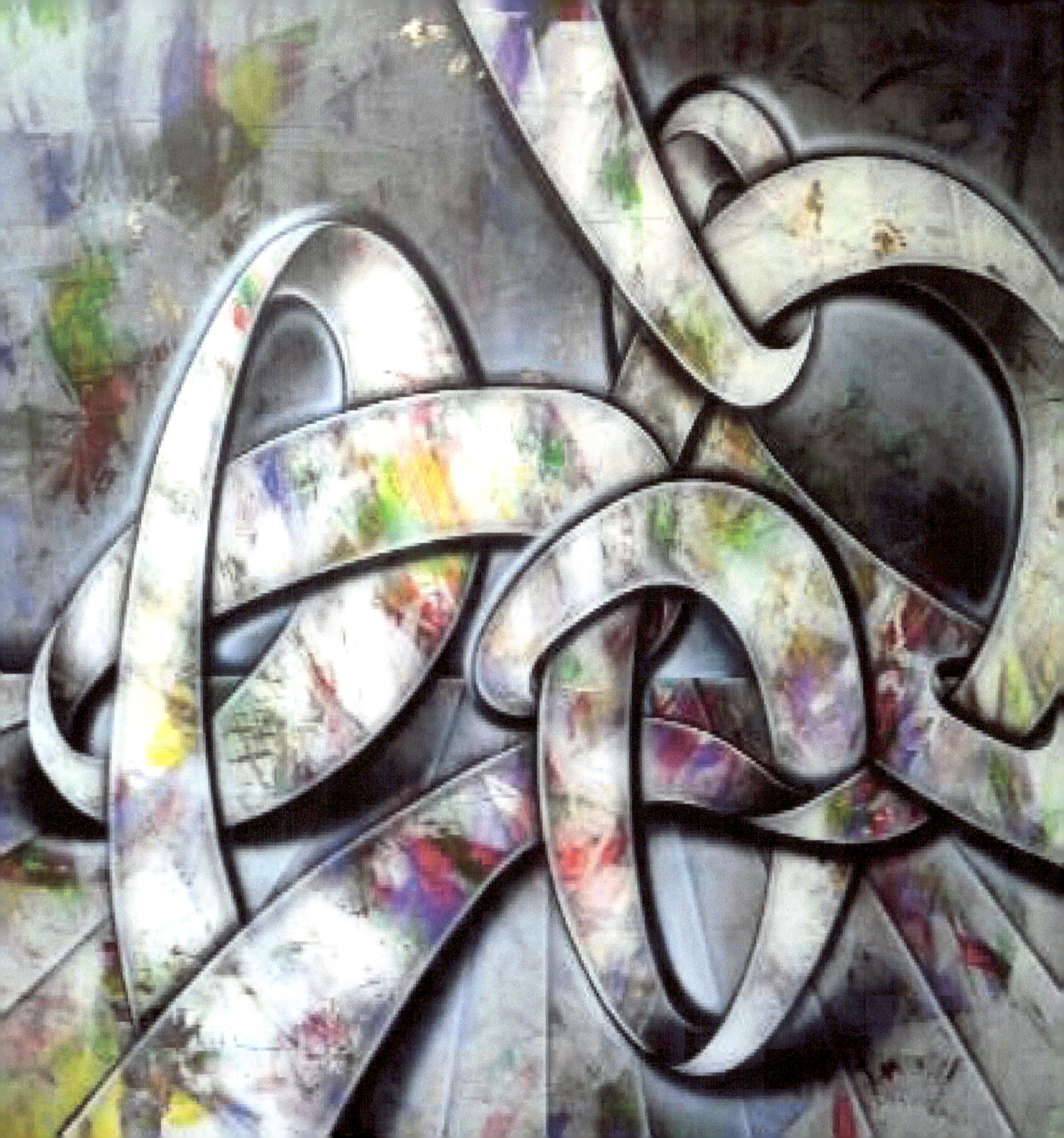

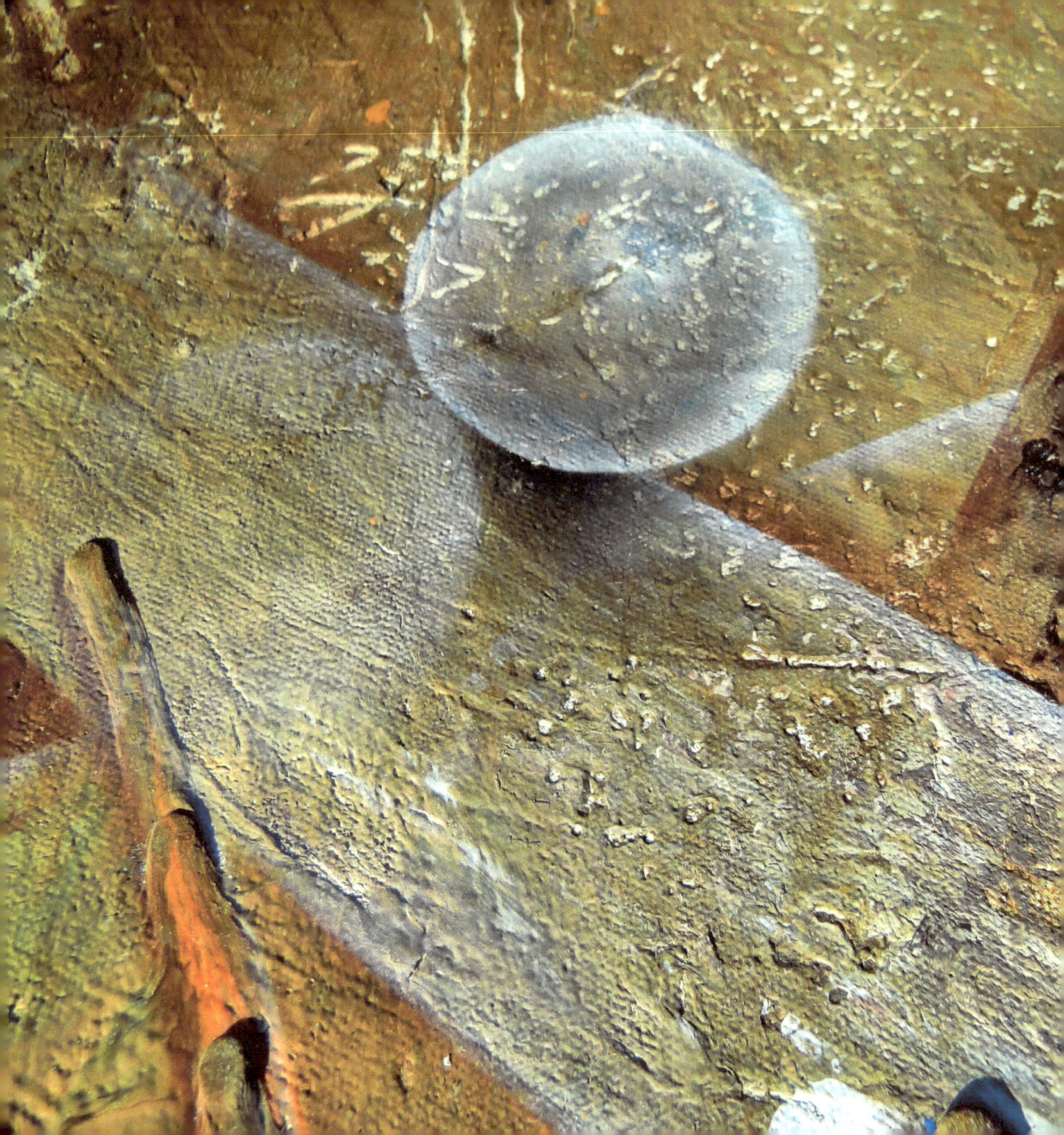

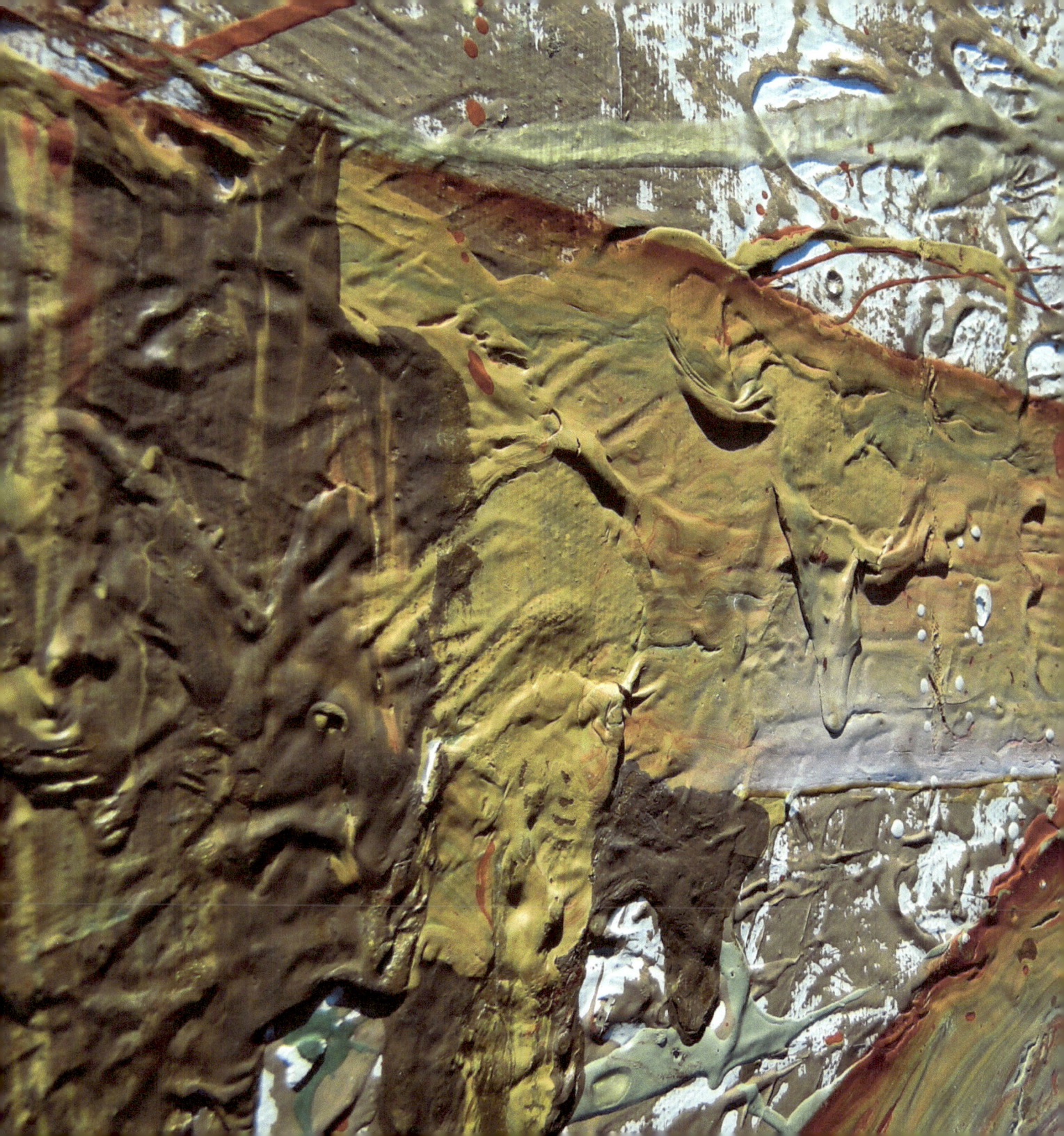

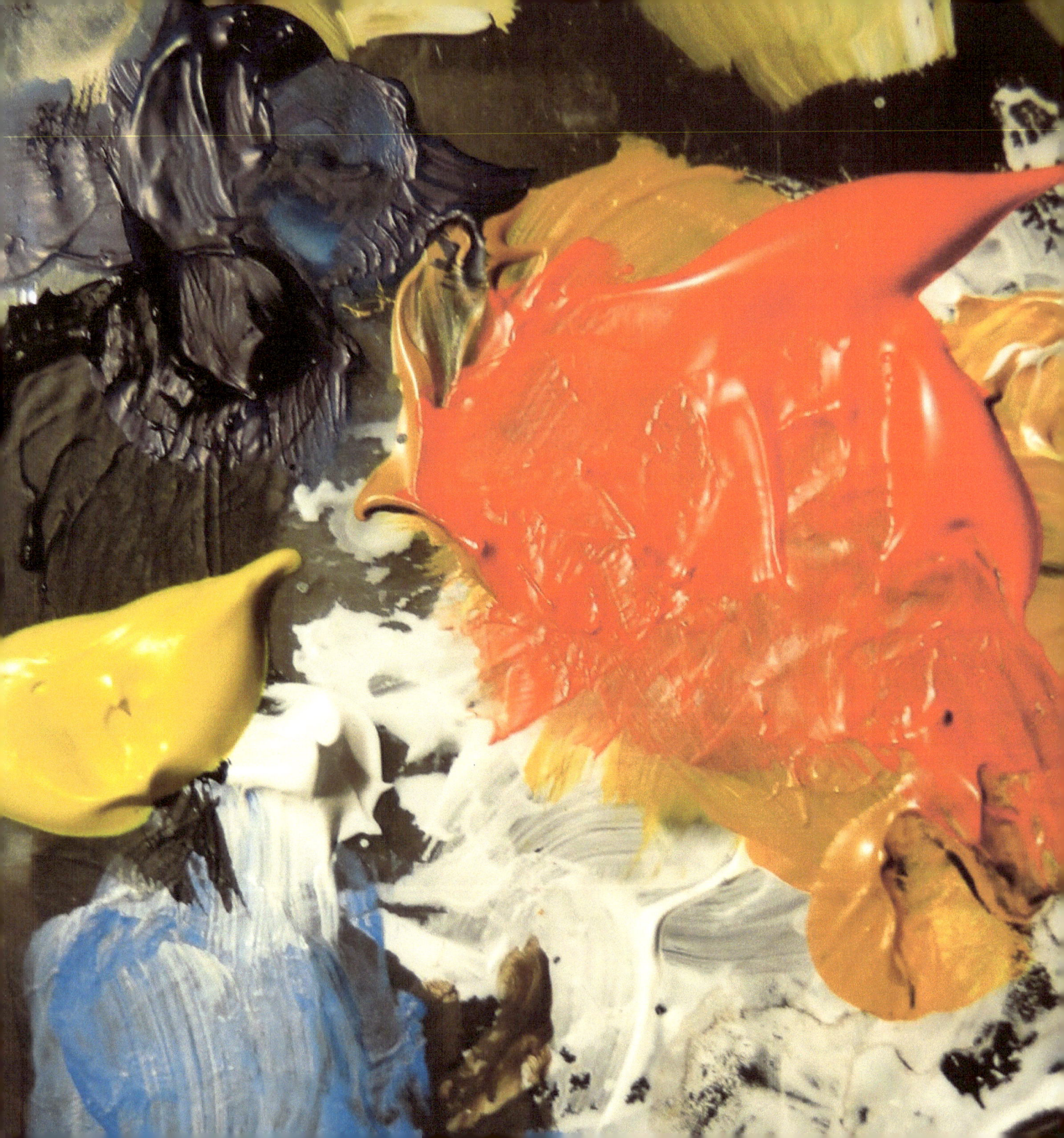

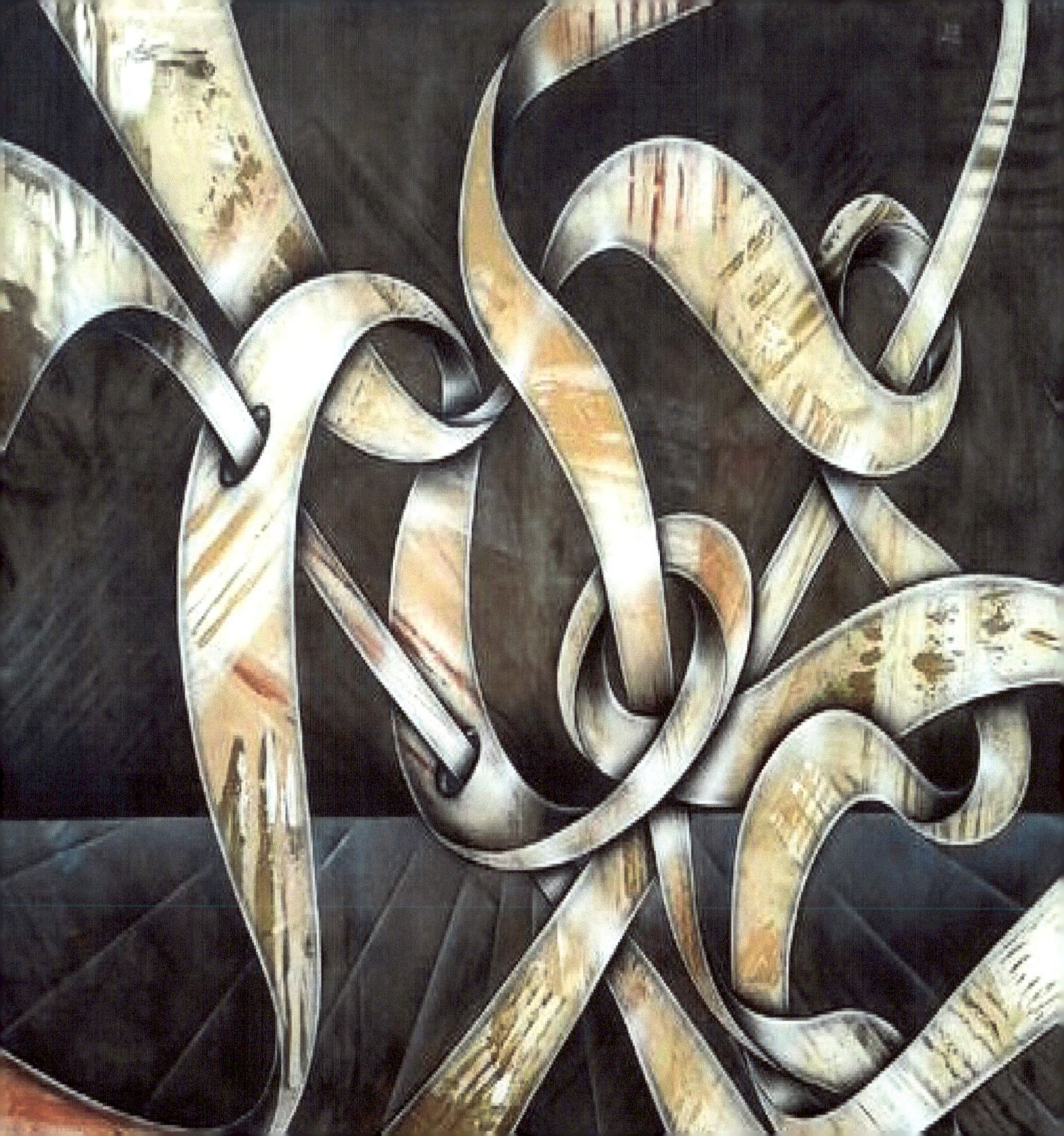

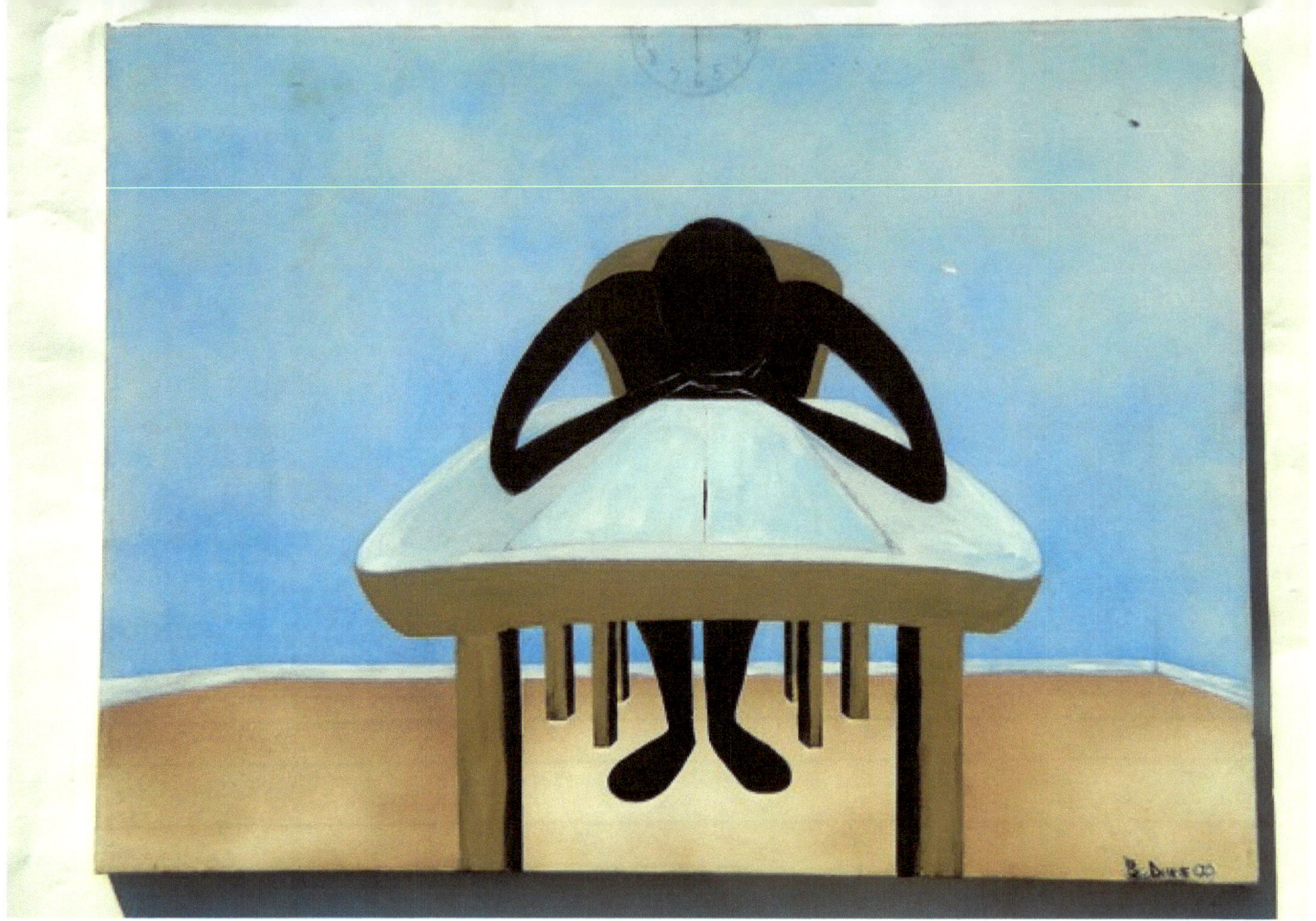

A painter took up his writing hand, and etched out the walk of man.

With his other one, he stopped to play some blues.

Then both started talking to my heart, as some jazz blended in with the hues.

"What's that line mean?" I pointed and asked.

He said, "That right there is the journey unmasked."

He told it in colors... how sweet it could be. He twisted the lines for all the paths I would see.

It made me think, and over time, I would find... He had also snapped a picture inside my mind.

"The Painter's Tale" by Gia'na Maya Garel

Life is a journey, survived by the lionhearted…

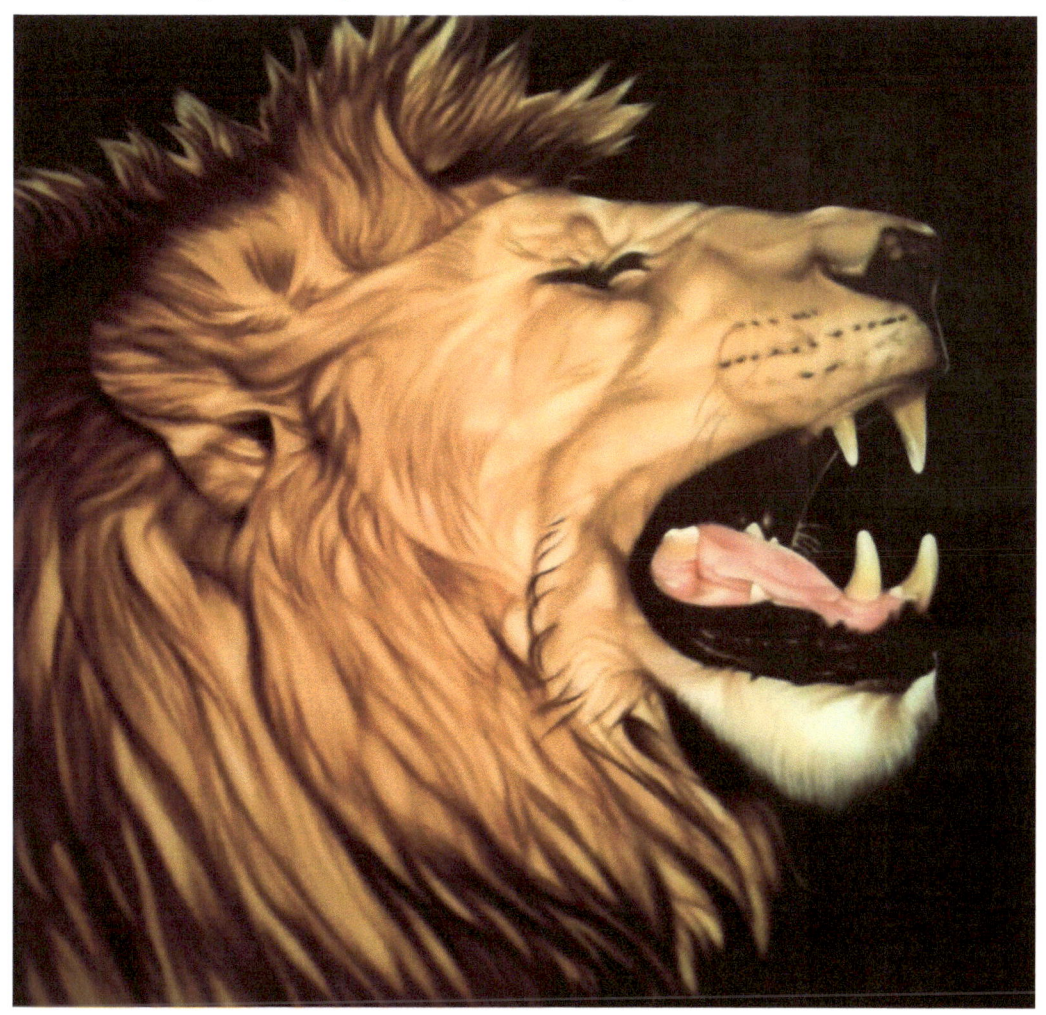

…and best enjoyed with a vivid imagination.

About The Author

Artist, Benjamin Allen brings over 34 years as a professional, self-taught painter. Recent clients have included the Tupac Shakur Museum in Atlanta, R&B legend Ronald Isley, The Isley Brothers, Russell Athletics, and murals featured on BRAVO Chnls seasons 1&2 - Married to Medicine; featuring a new children's Lego superhero mural in Mrs. Toya's sons' room. Allen is highly sought after for his 3D textured-to-the-touch portraits, his interior faux finishes, and other interior designs. He lives in Atlanta, Ga with his wife, poet Tammy Hillsman Allen. His next works include art themed children's book series, and collaborations of art and poetry with his wife.

www.ingramcontent.com/pod-product-compliance
Lightning Source LLC
Chambersburg PA
CBHW050859180526
45159CB00007B/2723